Layman's Bible Book Commentary
1 & 2 Kings, 2 Chronicles

LAYMAN'S BIBLE BOOK COMMENTARY

1 & 2 KINGS,
2 CHRONICLES
VOLUME 6

John H. Traylor, Jr.

BROADMAN PRESS
Nashville, Tennessee

To the members of my beloved congregation
Monroe's First Baptist Church
who inspire me to preach and
teach the Word of God
by their loving support of
my God-given ministry and
their hunger for the Word of life
and all it means.

© Copyright 1981 • Broadman Press.

4211-76

ISBN: 0-8054-1176-3

Dewey Decimal Classification: 222.5

Subject headings: BIBLE O. T. KINGS/BIBLE O. T. 2 CHRONICLES

Library of Congress Catalog Card Number: 80-67148

Printed in the United States of America

Foreword

The *Layman's Bible Book Commentary* in twenty-four volumes was planned as a practical exposition of the whole Bible for lay readers and students. It is based on the conviction that the Bible speaks to every generation of believers but needs occasional reinterpretation in the light of changing language and modern experience. Following the guidance of God's Spirit, the believer finds in it the authoritative word for faith and life.

To meet the needs of lay readers, the *Commentary* is written in a popular style, and each Bible book is clearly outlined to reveal its major emphases. Although the writers are competent scholars and reverent interpreters, they have avoided critical problems and the use of original languages except where they were essential for explaining the text. They recognize the variety of literary forms in the Bible, but they have not followed documentary trails or become preoccupied with literary concerns. Their primary purpose was to show what each Bible book meant for its time and what it says to our own generation.

The Revised Standard Version of the Bible is the basic text of the *Commentary*, but writers were free to use other translations to clarify an occasional passage or sharpen its effect. To provide as much interpretation as possible in such concise books, the Bible text was not printed along with the comment.

Of the twenty-four volumes of the *Commentary*, fourteen deal with Old Testament books and ten with those in the New Testament. The volumes range in pages from 140 to 168. Four major books in the Old Testament and five in the New are treated in one volume each. Others appear in various combinations. Although the allotted space varies, each Bible book is treated as a whole to reveal its basic message with some passages getting special attention. Whatever plan of Bible study the reader may follow, this *Commentary* will be a valuable companion.

Despite the best-seller reputation of the Bible, the average survey of Bible knowledge reveals a good deal of ignorance about it and its primary meaning. Many adult church members seem to think that its study

is intended for children and preachers. But some of the newer translations have been making the Bible more readable for all ages. Bible study
has branched out from Sunday into other days of the week, and into
neighborhoods rather than just in churches. This *Commentary* wants to
meet the growing need for insight into all that the Bible has to say about
God and his world and about Christ and his fellowship.

BROADMAN PRESS

Contents

1 and 2 KINGS

A United Kingdom Divides and Falls

2 Chronicles

The Deeds of the Kings of Judah from Solomon to the
Decree of Cyrus

1 & 2 KINGS

Introduction

Name and Position in Old Testament Canon

The two books now called 1 and 2 Kings were originally one book. The division into two books was first made in the third century BC by the seventy (or seventy-two) Jewish elders who translated the Hebrew Old Testament into Greek. That work was called the Septuagint, meaning "seventy," to designate the number of elders involved in the translation. The reason for their making Kings into two books is quite simple. The Hebrew manuscript, which, characteristically, contained no vowels, could be contained in one large scroll. The Greek translation with its vowels, however, required nearly twice as much space. The division, which interrupts the account of the reign of Ahaziah of Israel that had just begun, seems quite arbitrary.

These books, whose Hebrew title means "Kings," were listed by the Hebrews in the canon as The Former Prophets. The Former Prophets, which included Joshua, Judges, 1 and 2 Samuel, and 1 and 2 Kings, provide a prophetic interpretation of the history of Israel from the death of Moses to the Babylonian Exile. The translation of the Septuagint identified 1 and 2 Kings with 1 and 2 Samuel in naming these books respectively First, Second, Third, and Fourth Kingdom. All four books are appropriately called Books of the Kingdom, since 1 and 2 Samuel relate the establishment of the United Hebrew Kingdom, and 1 and 2 Kings tells of the division and fall of the Kingdom.

Authorship and Date

The text itself provides no definite statement concerning autnorship such as is found in words that are said to be the prophecies of Isaiah, Jeremiah, Ezekiel, and so forth. However, the perspective of the Books of Kings clearly mark them as the handiwork of the prophets. The Jewish Talmud says that Jeremiah wrote Jeremiah, Lamentations, and the Books of Kings. Jeremiah certainly could have written the bulk of the

Books of Kings. But the appendix that reports on the elevation of Jehoia-chin in the thirty-seventh year of his captivity in Babylon was written most likely by someone captive in Babylon. We know that Jeremiah was carried to Egypt where he probably died before the thirty-seventh year of Jehoiachin's captivity. Most Old Testament scholars mark the author(s) as a prophet who was a contemporary of Jeremiah and who lived and wrote during the reign of King Josiah, which was approximately 640-604 BC. Some are willing to attribute to him only the materials up to the death of Josiah. They credit an editor(s) who lived in the Babylonian captivity with the conclusion of the Book of Kings, which would be from the death of Josiah to the release of Jehoiachin in the thirty-seventh year of his reign (2 Kings 23:26 to 25:30).

Purpose and Enduring Value

The Books of Kings provide a prophetic interpretation of the history of Israel from the reign of Solomon to the thirty-seventh year of Jehoiachin in the Babylonian captivity to show that disobedience to God led to the division and fall of the United Hebrew Kingdom. If the bulk of the Kings material was indeed written by a prophet(s) during Josiah's reign, he doubtless used the material to encourage obedience to God as the only way for Judah to survive. As such, his prophetic interpretation of the history of Israel would have provided encouragement to Josiah and the people to turn back to God wholeheartedly in true worship, as reflected in the law of Moses. If the books were written or edited during the Baby-lonian captivity to include the fall of Judah, the author(s) and other prophets doubtless used the history to warn the Exilic and post-Exilic generations of the tragic consequences of disobedience to God. Espe-cially, they used the books to encourage the Israelites who would soon be brought back from captivity to establish themselves in the Land in full obedience to God. The "modern prophet" finds in these books divinely interpreted historical experiences by which he can call his nation back to God and encourage wholehearted devotion to God as the only way to build an enduring and blessed nation, society, church, family, and/or individual life.

Sources

To accomplish his purpose, the author(s) and/or editor(s) necessarily made use of certain sources. Three of these are mentioned by name as providing additional information for those desiring to investigate further the character and events of the reigns of the various kings: (1) the book of the acts of Solomon (1 Kings 11:41); (2) the Book of the Chronicles of the Kings of Israel (1 Kings 14:19; 15:31; and fifteen other references); and (3) the Book of the Chronicles of the Kings of Judah (1 Kings 14:29; 15:7; and thirteen other references). The latter two of these sources are not to be identified with the biblical Books of 1 and 2 Chronicles. These three sources were perhaps public annals kept by the official scribes of the various kings. However, more likely, these were documents prepared by the prophets much like Isaiah the prophet wrote concerning the acts of King Uzziah of Judah (2 Chron. 26:22). Other prophets identified as providing specific written records of this general time are: Nathan the prophet (2 Chron. 9:29); Ahijah the Shilonite (2 Chron. 9:29; Iddo the seer (2 Chron. 9:29; 12:15; 13:22); and Shemaiah the prophet (2 Chron. 12:15). Most scholars also believe that they see evidence of at least three other narratives that report on the outstanding prophets of the ninth and eighth centuries; namely, Elijah and Elisha of the Northern Kingdom and Isaiah of Judah. Some see 1 Kings 20 and 22 as reflecting a more positive source of the reign of Ahab than that found in the Elijah narratives. Also, there may have been additional sources such as priestly and Temple records that were utilized by the author(s) to produce the Books of Kings as we now have them.

Framework and Themes

As noted in the outline, the author(s) organized his prophetic history of Israel around the reigns of the various kings. Section 1 deals with the Hebrew kingdom in the days of Solomon and concludes with the division of the kingdom in the days of his son (1 Kings 1:1 to 12:24). Section 2 provides a synchronized account of the kings of Northern Israel and of Judah to the Fall of Israel (1 Kings 12:25 to 2 Kings 17:41). Section 3 delineates the Kingdom of Judah from the Fall of Israel to the Babylonian captivity with two appendixes reporting in the aftermath of Jerusalem's fall (2 Kings 18:1 to 25:30). A popular outline would be 1. The United Hebrew Kingdom; 2. The Divided Kingdom; and 3. Judah Alone.

To deal with the many events encompassing the approximately 413 years of Israel's history, the author utilized in each case an introductory and concluding formula and then included in between such events in the reign as he wished to describe. The introductory formula concerning the reign of Solomon occurs in 1 Kings 2:10-12 after the discussion of the last days of David, and the concluding formula is in 1 Kings 11:41-43.

The framework is especially seen in the synchronistic account of the kings of Northern Israel and of Judah. There the formula occurs for every king with monotonous regularity. Indeed, the author's intent on maintaining the framework was so strong that he applied it even to Zimri, who reigned only seven days (1 Kings 16:15-20). In the introductory formula for the kings of Northern Israel, the author included the following information: (1) the date of the King's accession in terms of the year of the reign of the king of Judah; (2) the length of the king's reign; and (3) the condemnation of the king for his walking in the ways of Jeroboam the son of Nebat. The name of the capital from which the king reigned is listed at times.

For the kings of Judah, the introductory formula is expanded to include: (1) often the age of the king when he began to reign; (2) the name of the queen mother and sometimes that of her father; and (3) a comparison with David, his forebear, in doing right in the eyes of the Lord. Only Hezekiah and Josiah are given unqualified approval (2 Kings 18:3; 22:2). Six other kings are given modified praise (1 Kings 15:14; 22:43; 2 Kings 12:2-3; 14:3-4; 15:3-4,34-35). The remaining ten kings are condemned because they did evil in the sight of the Lord (1 Kings 15:3; 2 Kings 8:18,27; 16:2; 21:2,20; 23:32,37; 24:9,19).

One cannot always tell why the author included the events he did to describe the reigns of the various kings. However, some themes are clearly seen. Certainly, he wanted to magnify the roles of certain great prophets. For example, he went into so much detail in the cases of Ahab and Hezekiah in order to focus on the roles of Elijah and Isaiah (1 Kings 16:29 to 22:40; 2 Kings 18:1 to 20:21). For the same reason, he interrupted the normal pattern of treating the reigns of the kings to include the large segment of material on Elisha (2 Kings 2:1 to 8:15).

Another purpose was to show how God blessed those kings who obeyed him and honored his house. Throughout, the author demonstrated that those who did good were blessed. A notable exception is the death of good King Josiah who was killed in battle by Neco, the king of Egypt (2 Kings 23:29). However, the later historian explained that Josiah died because he ignored the word of God that came to him through Neco (2 Chron. 35:20-23).

A third purpose was to show how the kingdom was divided and taken away in fulfillment of prophecy. Note the division of the kingdom in the days of Solomon's son (1 Kings 11:9-13,26-40; 12:21-33); the taking of the kingdom from the house of Jeroboam (1 Kings 14:7-17; 15:29); the taking of the kingdom from the house of Baasha (1 Kings 16:1-4,12); the taking of the kingdom from the house of Ahab (1 Kings 16:29-34; 20:42;

21:17-29; 22:37-38; 2 Kings 1:17; 9:24-26,36-37; 10:10-11,17); the taking of the kingdom from the house of Jehu (2 Kings 10:30-31; 15:12); the taking of the kingdom from all the seed of Israel (2 Kings 17:7-41, esp. vv. 20-23); and the taking of the kingdom from Judah (2 Kings 20:16-18; 21:10-15; 22:16-20; 23:26-27; 24:3-4,20; 25:21).

A fourth purpose was to demonstrate God's faithfulness in fulfilling his promise to David to establish his house and his throne forever (2 Sam. 7:12-17, esp. v. 16). The covenant with David was both certain and conditional. Disobedience on the part of David's descendants would result in chastisement, but not forfeiture of the covenant. Accordingly, God is seen to have maintained the descendants and the throne of David throughout. Note 1 Kings 2:1-4; 3:14; 9:1-9; 11:9-13,29-39; 12:20; 15:4-5; 2 Kings 8:16-19; 19:34; 20:6; 21:7-9. The divisions of the kingdom in the days of Solomon's son was an act of chastisement and not a permanent affliction (1 Kings 11:37-39). When wicked Athaliah sought to destroy all of David's descendants, God spared Joash and raised him to the throne of David (2 Kings 11:1-21). Even when the sin of Manasseh produced corruption in the people necessitating expulsion from the Land, God maintained the light of David in Exile. The gracious act of Evil-merodach in restoring the fortunes of Judah with which the author dramatically closes the Book of Kings illustrated the blessings of God still to come in his maintaining the descendants and throne of David forever (2 Kings 25:27-30).

The Hebrew Kingdom in the Days of Solomon and His Son

1:1 to 12:24

The Last Days of David (1:1 to 2:12)

David, who reigned from 1055-1015 BC, had anointed Solomon king and had made lavish preparations for Solomon to reign in his stead. David, however, became quite feeble in his last days (1:1-4) and allowed a political vacuum to be created into which Adonijah moved as heir-apparent to the throne (1:5-10). Quick action on the part of Nathan and Bathsheba stirred David to steps by which Solomon was reanointed and proclaimed to be king (1:11-40). When Adonijah saw Solomon's firm establishment as king (1:41-48), he feared for his life and submitted himself to Solomon (1:49-53). Following his final charge to his son Solomon (2:1-9), David died, and Solomon reigned as king (2:10-12).

David's Senility (1:1-4)

"Now" in the opening expression "Now King David" (v. 1) shows that 1 and 2 Kings are a continuation of 1 and 2 Samuel. King David was in his seventieth year (2 Sam. 5:4-5; 1 Kings 2:11). He had lost his vitality and was cold and uncomfortable. His servants made two attempts to keep him warm. One was to cover him with more clothing. When that failed, they selected a young and beautiful virgin named Abishag who hopefully by cherishing him would transfer her warmth and vitality to him. "Let her lie in your bosom" (v. 2) could mean that David's servants envisioned his having sexual relations with her. However, we're told that in that regard "the king knew her not" (v. 4). Abishag was considered as either a wife or a concubine of David (2:21-25). Although in violation of the marriage principle of one man for one woman (Gen. 2:24), polygamy was practiced in that day even by David, a man after God's own heart (1:2; 1 Sam. 13:14).

Adonijah's Plot to Be King (1:5-10)

Adonijah, the son of Haggith, was the fourth son of David and the oldest of those then living (2 Sam. 3:2-5). Accordingly, Adonijah had a claim on the throne as eldest son, and his commanding figure made him a popular choice of the people (v. 6b). God himself, however, chose the king of Israel (Deut. 17:15), and he had chosen Solomon to reign in David's stead (2 Sam. 12:24-25). Moreover, David had made Solomon king and proclaimed him as the one the Lord had chosen to sit upon David's throne and to build the house of God (1 Chron. 23:1; 28:2-8). Adonijah, however, was not willing to accept Solomon as the choice of the Lord and of David. His father David had failed to teach Adonijah to obey him and/or God, but had let him grow up free to grasp whatever he wanted, regardless of what was right (v. 6a).

Adonijah took three steps to make himself king. One was to prepare for himself a kingly entourage by which he declared his intention to be king and began to find out those who would support him (v. 5). His second step was to enlist the help of Joab, who had been David's chief military leader, and of Abiathar, who had shared with Zadok the high priesthood in the reign of David (v. 7). Joab had been marked by David for death, and Joab doubtless supported Adonijah in the hope of preserving his life and of keeping himself in power. Adonijah's third step was the proclamation feast which was held at Enrogel, a fountain outside of Jerusalem just below the junction of the Kidron and Hinnom valleys (v. 9). The exclusion of Solomon and his supporters from the proclamation feast indicated that Adonijah was well aware of the proclaimed intentions of the Lord and of David that Solomon was to be David's successor (v. 10).

Nathan's Announcement and Charge to Bathsheba (1:11-27)

Nathan and Bathsheba blocked Adonijah's bid for the throne with their counteraction to affirm Solomon's kingship. First, Nathan told Bathsheba of Adonijah's plot and charged her to speak with King David about reaffirming Solomon as king (vv. 11-14). Second, Bathsheba alerted David to Adonijah's plot and exhorted David to reaffirm Solomon as king (vv. 15-21). Third, Nathan confirmed to King David Adonijah's usurpation of the throne and tacitly encouraged David to take charge of Solomon's reaffirmation as king (vv. 22-27).

David's Action by Which Solomon Was Made King (1:28-40)

David's response shows that he was stirred by Nathan and Bathsheba to mental and spiritual alertness. He reaffirmed to Bathsheba his pledge to make Solomon king (vv. 28-31). Although we do not have any record of the oath of David to Bathsheba to make Solomon king, David acknowledged the oath and swore by the living God who had chosen Solomon as his successor to take action that day to establish Solomon as king. "He" in the expression "he shall sit upon my throne" (v. 30; see 1:13,17) is emphatic, so as to carry the meaning of Solomon and no other.

True to his oath, David assembled Zadok the priest, Nathan the prophet, and Benaiah the captain of the king's guard and issued to them instructions for making Solomon king (vv. 32-37). "The servants of your lord" (v. 33) were the king's guard, identified as the Cherethites and Pelethites (v. 38). Etymologically, the Cherethites and the Pelethites are identified respectively with the Cretans and the Philistines, as is noted by the similarities of the radicals. The Cherethites inhabited the southern portion of the land of the Philistines (1 Sam. 30:14). "The Cherethites and the Pelethites" were a group of Philistines that David made his personal bodyguard during the time of his exile in that land. Although his personal bodyguard retained its original titles, it was probably made up now of trusted soldiers recruited at large from all his subjects. Their presence with Solomon would weigh heavily for him in the power struggle for the throne.

David's instructions called for Zadok, Nathan, and Benaiah first to organize and bring to Gihon a royal procession with Solomon riding upon David's mule (v. 33). Gihon, which means "a bursting forth," was a gushing spring (known today as Virgin's Fount) on the eastern side of Jerusalem at the foot of Ophel. Gihon was north of and out of sight of, but within hearing distance of Enrogel, where Adonijah was involved in his coronation feast. Second, Zadok and Nathan, as the divinely appointed representatives of God, were to anoint Solomon at Gihon to be king over Israel (v. 34a). The act of anointing, which involved pouring or smearing oil upon Solomon's head, symbolized Solomon's divine ordination to the office of king, his God-given power to accomplish his duties as king, and his divinely-protected opportunity to fulfill his office. Third, they were to blow the trumpet and shout, "Long live King Solomon," in order publicly to announce Solomon's establishment as king (v. 34b). Finally, they were to lead the royal procession to the throne of David where Solomon would occupy the throne in David's stead (v. 35). Benaiah expressed the approval of himself, Zadok, and Nathan to David's plan (vv. 36-37), and then they faithfully carried out his instructions to make Solomon king (vv. 38-40).

Adonijah's Submission of Himself to Solomon's Rule (1:41-53)

News of Solomon's establishment as king spread quickly to Adonijah and his party (vv. 41-48). All of Adonijah's supporters feared and fled for their lives (v. 49). Adonijah himself sought refuge at the horns of the altar (v. 50). Solomon did grant Adonijah conditional impunity (vv. 51-52), and Adonijah submitted himself to Solomon's rule (v. 53).

David's Final Charge to Solomon (2:1-9)

From his deathbed (v. 1), David delivered to Solomon a fourfold charge: (1) to keep God's charge to walk in the ways of the Lord as written in the law of Moses (vv. 2-4); (2) to avenge the blood of Abner and Amasa by putting to death Joab their murderer (vv. 5-6); (3) to reward with steadfast kindness the loyalty to David of the sons of Barzillai (v. 7); and (4) to avenge the curse of Shimei by putting him to death (vv. 8-9). Joab murdered Abner and Amasa in cold blood (2 Sam. 3:22-27; 20:4-10). Since David was sovereign and responsible for avenging their deaths, their unrequited blood was on his girdle (v. 5). He could not expect his dynasty to be blessed of God apart from obedience to God's command to execute wrath upon a murderer. Shimei's cursing of David as God's anointed was a capital offense in the same category as reviling God (Ex. 22:28; 1 Kings 21:9-10). "Grievous" (v. 8) indicates that David looked upon Shimei's curse as an infectious germ that would weaken and cripple his dynasty unless removed.

David's Death and Solomon's Accession (2:10-12)

David, after a reign of forty years and six months, was buried in the stronghold of Zion, which had been renamed in his honor "the city of David" (2 Sam. 5:4,7). "Solomon" (v. 12) is emphatic and indicates that, according to the providence of God, Solomon and no other had been established as David's successor.

The Reign of Solomon: The Seed of Division (2:13 to 11:43)

The reign of Solomon (1015 to 975 BC) was a time of unprecedented glory for the kingdom of Israel. However, Solomon's glory stemmed mainly from the blessings of God upon him for David's sake, rather than for Solomon's own personal goodness. Although Solomon "loved the Lord" (3:3), his devotion was tainted by disobedience that expressed itself early in his marriage to an Ammonite, in his marriage to Pharaoh's daughter, and in his worship of the Lord in forbidden places (14:21; 3:1,3). In his later life, his disobedience led to his apostasy which caused the kingdom to be divided in the days of his son (11:1-13; 12:16-20). Solomon's sin cast a spell of doom across his wisdom, wealth, and building achievements.

Solomon's Purge of His Enemies (2:13-46)

Solomon further established his reign at the death of David by purging his enemies. Solomon killed Adonijah (2:13-25), exiled Abiathar to Anathoth (2:26-27), and slew Joab (2:28-34). He replaced Joab with Benaiah and Abiathar with Zadok (2:35). Moreover, Solomon restricted Shimei to Jerusalem and then killed Shimei for violating the restriction (2:36-46).

Although Bathsheba apparently thought Adonijah's request for Abishag to be innocent, Solomon rightly interpreted it as another move in the part of Adonijah to take the throne (v. 22). Possessing the former king's harem was a sign of his possession of the throne (2 Sam.

16:21-22). Solomon's exile of Abiathar was interpreted as fulfillment of Samuel's prophecy that the family of Eli to which Abiathar belonged would be cut off from the priest's office (v. 27; 1 Sam. 2:31-36). The horns of the altar were the most sacred portion of the altar, inasmuch as the blood of the sacrifice was placed there as a sign of atonement for sin (Ex. 29:12; 30:10). In laying hold upon the horns of the altar (v. 28), Joab sought to place himself under God's protection and pleaded for God's grace to wipe away his sin and punishment. The law did allow for one guilty of unintentional manslaughter to plead sanctuary from the avenger by laying hold upon the altar; however, the law made no provision of mercy for a cold-blooded murderer (Ex. 21:12-14). Accordingly, Solomon executed Joab even while Joab pleaded for mercy.

Solomon's Love for God Tainted (3:1-3)

The overall testimony of this passage is to Solomon's love for the Lord. Indeed, Solomon would appear on the surface to have rivaled his father David as a man after God's own heart. However, the word "only" (v. 3), which means "except" or "but," clearly denotes that Solomon's love for God was tainted by his worship of God in the high places. Also, his marriage to Pharaoh's daughter, which appears innocent enough, was actually a political and military alliance by which he could have access to Egyptian chariots (v. 1). Such an alliance was expressly forbidden by God because it would lead the king and the people of Israel to trust in chariots rather than in the Lord (Deut. 17:16). Solomon was already married in violation of God's command to Naamah the Ammonitess and had by her his son Rehoboam, who succeeded him (14:21; 11:2,42).

The high places were the altars that had been erected by the Canaanites to their pagan gods, and at which they conducted all sorts of licentious rites. The Lord commanded the Israelites to tear down these altars and to worship him only at the designated place (Deut. 12:1-14). The proper place of worship had been obscured by the sins of the people. Joshua, in obedience to God's command, established the tabernacle of Moses at Shiloh (Josh. 18:1). There the tabernacle remained until the war with the Philistines during the last days of Eli the priest. The ark was carried before the army of Israel into battle against the Philistines in the false hope that it would bring them victory (1 Sam. 4:3-4). The ark, however, was captured by the Philistines and remained among them for a season until it was returned to Kiriath-jearim (1 Sam. 7:1-2). Samuel the prophet led the people in worship and judged them at such sites as

Mizpah, Bethel, Gilgal, and Ramah, apparently at altars he himself erected to the Lord (1 Sam. 7:16-17). We next hear of the tabernacle minus the ark at Nob where it was cared for by Ahimelech the priest (1 Sam. 21:1). Saul, however, put Ahimelech and other priests to death for aiding David (1 Sam. 22:11 ff.). Saul then presumably moved the tabernacle without the ark to the high place at Gibeon (1 Chron. 16:39; 21:29). Presumably, this high place was a pagan altar which had been converted for the worship of the Lord.

When David captured the city of Jerusalem, he moved the ark there from Kiriath-jearim and made for it another tent (1 Chron. 13:5,13-14; 15:1; 16:1). However, he left the original tabernacle with its altar at Gibeon (2 Chron. 1:3-6). Then David was told by the Lord that the place of the permanent abode of the ark and the altar of sacrifice was to be at the threshing floor of Ornan the Jebusite (1 Chron. 21:18; 22:1). It appears that Solomon should have offered his sacrifices to God at this altar where he was later to build the house of God. In any case, his sacrifice to God at pagan altars was marked as a deviation from his pure love for God. His marriage of the Ammonite woman, his worship of God at the high places, and his marriage to Pharaoh's daughter were the seeds of disobedience that reached their full flower in his later sins of marrying many foreign women and worshiping their gods in the high places (11:1-8).

God's Appearance to Solomon at Gibeon (3:4-15)

Solomon offered his large-scale sacrifices at Gibeon to ask God to bless his reign and to make clear to the people his great love of God (v. 4). In response, God appeared to Solomon in a dream vision and told Solomon to ask of him whatever he wanted (v. 5). Solomon praised God for his faithfulness in establishing him as king and requested an understanding heart to judge the people (vv. 6-9). God promised to give Solomon an understanding heart and also riches and honor (vv. 10-13). God, however, warned Solomon of the need to be obedient if Solomon were to enjoy length of days both in life and in the Land (v. 14). Solomon awoke from his dream vision, returned to Jerusalem, and there before the ark of the Lord worshiped in thanksgiving for his promised blessing (v. 15). Solomon is rightly praised for his request for an understanding heart. However, he fell short in not asking God to give to him also a loyal and righteous heart, which would keep him in the way of the Lord (v. 14). In response to the question as to why God did not give him a loyal and righteous heart along with understanding, riches, and honor, it must be said that certain things cannot be given if we do not want them. You can't, for example, give your child a college education if he does not desire it. You can pay his expenses, perhaps even make him go to class, but you cannot make him learn if he does not desire to do so.

Solomon's Reign in Wisdom, Wealth, and Glory (3:16 to 4:34)

Generally speaking, the purpose of this section is to illustrate that God faithfully kept his promise to give Solomon wisdom, riches, and glory. The experience of the two harlots illustrates that God gave to Solomon an understanding heart (3:16-28). His exercise of his God-given wisdom resulted in his being established as king throughout all Israel in the minds of the people (4:1). Their "awe of the king" (3:28) involved both fear and reverence, for they detected in his judicial decisions a super-human ability to determine truth and falsehood and to punish evildoers.

Solomon also had administrative genius. His chief officers are listed in 4:1-6 and his district officials in 4:7-19. The notation that "Azariah the son of Zadok" (4:2) was priest indicates that the list refers to a time later in Solomon's reign inasmuch as Zadok himself was high priest at the beginning of Solomon's reign. Abiathar (4:4) apparently refers to the high priest Solomon deposed in favor of Zadok (2:26-27). "Secretaries" (4:3) were keepers of official documents. "Recorder" (4:3) means the one who caused the king to remember by calling matters to his attention. Azariah (v. 5) was chief tax collector in charge of the district tax collectors mentioned in verses 7-19. "King's friend" (v. 5) means special companion and counselor. Many question the wisdom of Solomon's forced labor policies and his heavy taxation to keep his elaborate court system in provisions.

Solomon's glory is reflected in the extent, well-being, security, and wealth of his reign (4:20-28). Solomon's daily provisions (vv. 22-23) illustrate the staggering amount each district officer was required to provide for his month of the year (4:7). Solomon's glory was especially reflected in his personal wisdom, which exceeded all other men of his day (4:29-31), which enabled him to produce proverbs and songs and to speak with wisdom concerning botany and biology (4:32-33), and which gave him worldwide fame (4:34).

Solomon's Building of the House of the Lord (5:1 to 6:38)

Solomon understood and was in sympathy with his God-given task of building the house of the Lord. Accordingly, as soon as he had consolidated his kingdom, Solomon began to make preparation to begin the work. First, he negotiated with Hiram, king of Tyre—the longtime friend of his father—to secure the necessary building materials (5:1-12). Chief among the materials were cedar and cypress wood (5:6,8,10). A "cor" (5:11) was 5.16 bushels or 55 gallons. "The beaten oil" (5:11) was pure olive oil obtained by crushing olives in a hand mortar.

Second, Solomon provided laborers and materials from his own kingdom to build the house of God (5:13-18). The "levy of forced labor" (5:13) was much like our draft for military service. Those chosen had to give their labor. The Israelites were usually exempt from Solomon's forced labor program, which was reserved for those Canaanites who dwelt in the Land (9:21-22). However, the thirty thousand seem to be free Israelites who were conscripted to work alongside the men of Hiram. The program of one month in Lebanon and two months at home made the labor less severe (5:14). The "burden-bearers" (5:15) and "hewers of stone" (5:15) and "chief officers" (5:16) who worked in the limestone hills of Palestine were probably Canaanites on whom was forced permanent slavery. Comparison of these numbers with those given in 1 Kings 9:23, 2 Chronicles 2:18, and 8:10 seems to suggest that Solomon had a total of 3,850 overseers of whom 3,300 were Canaanite lesser overseers, 300 were superior Canaanite overseers, and 250 were Israelite chief overseers. "The men of Gebal" (5:18) were natives of the ancient Phoenician city called "Byblos" by the Greeks and were doubtless especially skilled builders among Hiram's force.

The time of the beginning of the actual construction of the house of God is described from two viewpoints (6:1). First, the work was begun 480 years after Moses led the Israelites out of Egypt. Second, it was begun in the fourth year of Solomon's reign on the second day of the second month of the Hebrew calendar, which would be roughly speaking our May/June. The beginning of Solomon's reign is fixed at approximately 975 BC, which would date the Exodus at approximately 1455 BC. The Temple was built in Mount Moriah on the threshing floor of Ornan the Jebusite at the place appointed by David (2 Chron. 3:1).

A general description of the house of God is given in 6:2-10. The plan, which was given to Solomon by David, was revealed to David by God. Indeed, David claimed that God himself wrote the plan on his heart (1 Chron. 28:19). God, however, seemed less than anxious, at least initially, for the house to be built (2 Sam. 7:4-7).

The house was exactly twice the size of the tabernacle. Figuring the cubit as eighteen inches, it was ninety feet long, thirty feet wide, and forty-five feet high (6:2). It faced east like the tabernacle with the holy place comprising the eastern sixty feet (6:17) and the holy of holies comprising the western thirty feet (6:16). Attached to the front of the house was a vestibule or porch thirty feet wide and fifteen feet long, making the total length of the structure one hundred and five feet (6:3). The Temple had a three-storied chamber for sleeping quarters built around its north, west, and south walls that extended upward a total of twenty-two and one-half feet (6:5). The walls of the Temple then rose twenty-two and one-half feet higher, and in that space there were windows in the walls of the holy place (6:4). Each story of the side chambers was one cubit wider than the one below it (6:6). The house itself was built of stones made ready at the quarry (6:7), with its ceilings made of cedar beams and planks (6:9) and its floors of cypress boards (6:15).

In the midst of the construction of the Temple, God once again set forth the condition of obedience for his presence in his house (6:11-13). "Concerning this house which you are building" is emphatic. The Temple had no magical value to bring God's blessings. It had value only as it symbolized their love and obedience to God. The promise to which God referred was to the everlasting establishment of David's throne (2 Sam. 7:12-17). Each generation would of necessity stand at the crossroads. David, as a man after God's own heart, possessed the Land for himself and his generation and gave it to Solomon his son for an everlasting inheritance. Solomon in turn had by his own obedience to God to possess the Land for himself and his generation and to give it to his children for an eternal inheritance. God's dwelling among them and not forsaking them provided special application of the promise to Solomon and to the Israelites of his day. Note that God did not say that he would dwell simply in his house, but "among" his people. Already the concept was established of God's dwelling in the hearts of his people and imparting to them his personal glory (Ex. 29:43-46). As it turned out, the glory of Solomon's Temple was short-lived. Because of his sin, it was plundered five years after his death (1 Kings 14:25-26). Continued sin of the kings and the people led to its destruction in 586 BC. The description of God's house is continued in 6:14-36. The cedar walls in the holy place were carved with floral designs (vv. 18,29). Since the holy of holies was a cube of thirty feet, steps perhaps went upward from the holy place to the most holy place that housed the ark of the covenant (v. 20). The "altar of cedar" (v. 20) was the altar of incense and probably was of cedar wood overlaid with gold. It was placed in the holy place before the veil that separated the holy place from the holy of holies (v. 20). The "chains of gold" (v. 21) were probably used to fasten the doors separating the holy of holies (v. 31).

The two cherubim were made of olivewood and overlaid with pure gold, each being fifteen feet high and each having a wing span of fifteen feet (vv. 23-28). The cherubim, whose function was to guard the presence of God, were placed in the holy of holies to face eastward with their wings touching. Perhaps, as suggested by archaeology, they had heads of humans and bodies of lions. The doors of the holy of holies were of olivewood in the shape of a pentagon with carvings of cherubim and floral designs overlaid with gold (vv. 31-32). The folding doors to the holy place were of cypress wood also with carvings of cherubims and floral designs overlaid with gold (vv. 33-35). Solomon built the inner court of the Temple with hewn stone and cedar beams (v. 36). This is the area known as "the court of the priests," in contrast with "the great court" where the people came (2 Chron. 4:9). Although no dimensions of these courts are given, the size for the Temple courts can be estimated following the analogy of the tabernacle as 300 feet long and 150 feet wide for the court of the priests and 600 feet long and 300 feet wide for the great court.

Seven years were required to build the house of God (6:37-38). Solomon laid the foundation in the second month of the fourth year of his reign and completed it in the eighth month of the eleventh year of his reign, which would be roughly speaking in the year 1004/1003 BC.

Solomon's Building of His Own Elaborate Palace (7:1-12)

"His own house" (v. 1) refers to the palace complex which included the House of the Forest of Lebanon (vv. 2-5), the Hall of Pillars (v. 6), the Hall of the Throne (v. 7), his own house (v. 8a), and the house for Pharaoh's daughter (v. 9b). Verses 9-12 describe the materials used in building the palace and the great court. The House of the Forest of Lebanon, which also served as the armory (10:17), was named for the elaborate use of cedar in its construction. The Hall of Pillars, which seemed to have been a canopied porch with pillars, perhaps served as an entrance to the Hall of the Throne where Solomon sat to render judgment. The thirteen years required to build his palace were in addition to the seven years required to build the house of God, so that Solomon spent a total of twenty years building the house of the Lord and his palace (1 Kings 9:10). The longer time required to build the palace was due to its being larger than the Temple, plus the years of preparation that preceded the actual building of the Temple. However, the expression "But Solomon was building his own house thirteen years" (7:1, KJV) seems to point up another flaw in Solomon's armor—that of building for himself more magnificently than for God.

Metalwork for the House of the Lord (7:13-51)

A distinction must be made between Hiram the king of Tyre and Hiram the metalworker whom the king of Tyre sent to do the metalwork for the house of the Lord (2 Chron. 2:13). Hiram the metalworker was one-half Israelite, his father being a Tyrian bronze worker and his mother an Israelite who was herself of the tribe of Dan and a widow of a man of the tribe of Naphtali (v. 14; 2 Chron. 2:14). Hiram, who had magnificent ability for any work in bronze, did all of the metalwork for Solomon. Included were the two pillars of bronze (vv. 15-22), the altar of bronze (2 Chron. 4:1), the molten sea (vv. 23-26), the ten bronze stands (vv. 27-37), the ten bronze lavers (v. 38), the pots, shovels, and basins (vv. 40-47), and the smaller Temple vessels and the doors (vv. 48-50). He cast the larger vessels out of bronze and the smaller vessels and doors out of gold. Of special interest, mainly because of their names, are the two pillars of bronze that were placed on either side of the vestibule (v. 21). "Jachin" means "he shall cause to be established," and "Boaz" means "in strength." "Jachin" is the same root used by God in his promise to establish David's dynasty forever. Taken together the pillars meant to Solomon that he could cause his dynasty to be established forever in the strength of the worship of God symbolized by the Temple. "The molten sea," which was placed on the southeast corner of the house, was used for the priests to wash themselves (v. 39; 2 Chron. 4:6). The bronze lavers on their stands, which were placed five on the south side and five on the north side of the house, served to wash the utensils used for the burnt offering (2 Chron. 4:6). When King Solomon had completed all the work on the house of the Lord, he brought into the treasury of the house the booty and gifts provided by David (v. 51).

Solomon's Dedication of the House of the Lord (8:1 to 8:66)

Solomon dedicated the house of the Lord in conjunction with the Feast of the Tabernacles in the twelfth year of his reign, eleven months after the Temple was completed (8:2). Actually, they held the dedication ceremonies for seven days and then the Feast of Tabernacles for seven days (2 Chron. 7:8-9). In keeping with the Feast of Tabernacles, branches were used by the Israelites to make booths in which they dwelt in Jerusalem for the fourteen-day period. The purpose of the Feast of Tabernacles, which began on the fifteenth day of the seventh month at the time of the ingathering of the crop, was to remind the Israelites that their forefathers dwelt in tents when God brought them out of the land of Egypt (Lev. 23:34-39,43). Perhaps the Feast of Tabernacles was linked with the dedication ceremonies to contrast the tabernacle as the dwelling place of God among his people who had no land with the Temple as the permanent dwelling place of God among his people now living in the Promised Land. Dedication activities included depositing the ark in its place in the holy of holies under the wings of the cherubim (8:1-13), Solomon's address to the assembly of Israel (8:14-21), his dedicatory prayer (8:22-53), his blessing and exhortation of the assembly of Israel (8:54-61), and their dedicatory sacrifices (8:62-64).

The ark, which was made by Bezalel at the instructions of Moses (Ex. 25:10-12), contained only the two tables of stone on which God himself wrote the Ten Commandments (8:9). These tables bore witness to the moral demands of the covenant. Since the two tables were kept in the ark, it was called the ark of the covenant or the ark of testimony (8:1; Ex. 26:34). When the priests came out of the house of God where they had put the ark in its place, the glory of God shrouded by cloud filled the Temple, symbolizing that God himself had taken up his permanent abode in his house (8:10-11). It was understood that his presence was above the ark of the covenant with his feet separated from the tables of testimony by the mercy seat. There the glorious God, who demanded and gave holiness to his people, met with them in mercy. Solomon's response reflected his amazement (1) that the glorious God had taken up his abode among his people as promised; and (2) that he had had the privilege of building the house in which God would dwell among them forever (8:12-13).

In his dedicatory prayer, Solomon praised and invoked the Lord as the covenant keeping God (8:22-26), asked that the house of God always be the place to which Israel could turn to God to seek his forgiveness (8:27-30), and asked God specifically to hear and answer concerning seven petitions (8:31-53). Solomon underscored his understanding that God could not be contained in the house he had built for him. Although God's dwelling place is in heaven (8:30), even the heaven of heavens cannot contain him. God is everywhere. Yet he had chosen to set his name in his house, making it the special place where he would meet with his people to teach them his way, to accept their sacrifices, to forgive their sins, and to enjoy their worship. When Solomon concluded his dedicatory prayer, the fire of God's presence came down from heaven and consumed the burnt offerings and sacrifices, and the glory of the Lord once again filled the Temple in visible manifestation (2 Chron. 7:1). By these acts, God confirmed that he had hallowed the Temple as the place of sacrifice and prayer, that he had accepted the people on the basis of the prescribed sacrifices and their consecration to him, and that he would dwell among them in the Temple. At the conclusion of the dedication ceremonies and the Feast of Tabernacles, Solomon blessed the people, and they returned to their homes joyful for the goodness of God shown to the dynasty of David and to his people (8:66).

God Appeared to Solomon: Conditional Promises and Warnings (9:1-9)

Shortly after the twenty years of Solomon's reign required to build the house of God and Solomon's palace (9:1-2,10), God appeared to Solomon a second time in a dream vision, as he had appeared to him at Gibeon at the beginning of Solomon's reign. The appearance was perhaps occasioned by Solomon's slipping deeper and deeper into sin. God first spoke with Solomon concerning the house of God that Solomon had built and had consecrated to God nine years previously. God reminded him that he had heard his prayer for the house of God, that he had consecrated the house of God as the place of worship, and that he had set his name there forever (v. 3). But God also reminded Solomon that God's blessings upon him and his children, upon the house of God, and upon the nation of Israel were dependent upon their obedience to God (vv. 4-9). If Solomon would walk before God, God would establish forever on the throne of Israel the line of Solomon as well as the line of David (vv. 4-5). Implied is that the obedience of Solomon and his descendants to God would also result in God's house and God's people being blessed and a source of blessing. But if Solomon and/or his children turned aside from following God, then God would cut Israel off from the Land, cast out of his sight the house consecrated to his name, and make exiled Israel and the devastated house of God a proverb concerning what happens to disobedient servants of God (vv. 6-9).

Further Details of Solomon's Magnificence (9:10 to 10:29)

This section provides the account of Solomon's sale of twenty cities to Hiram (9:10-14), of Solomon's forced labor for his vast building projects (9:15-23), of Solomon's moving Pharaoh's daughter to her new residence and the building of Millo (9:24), of Solomon's regular sacrifices at the house of the Lord (9:25), of Solomon's naval enterprises in the Red Sea (9:26-29), of his being visited by the Queen of Sheba (10:1-13), of his wealth (10:14-22), and a summary of Solomon's riches, wisdom, military might, and honor (10:23-29).

Solomon's Apostasy and Punishment (11:1-40)

God's warnings failed to turn Solomon back to God. Solomon began his reign worshiping God at forbidden altars and seeking military power by marrying Pharaoh's daughter. He ended up in his old age loving many heathen women and in worshiping pagan gods in high places he himself built for this worship by his wives (vv. 4-5).

Solomon's apostasy is described in verses 1-8. Solomon loved and took for wives and concubines many foreign women besides the daughter of Pharaoh. Remember that Solomon's son and successor Rehoboam was of Solomon's Ammonite wife Naamah (14:21). Here Moabite, Ammonite, Edomite, Sidonian, and Hittite women are mentioned as being among his seven hundred wives and three hundred concubines. Marriage with these women was forbidden a king of Israel and indeed any Israelites, lest they turn the hearts of their husbands (and children born to their union) away from the Lord God of Israel to pagan deities (v. 2; Deut. 7:3-5). That's exactly what happened in Solomon's case.

Solomon himself followed Ashtoreth, Milcom, and Chemosh (vv. 5,33). Ashtoreth, the Sidonian fertility goddess, was the consort of Baal. She was known to the Babylonians and the Assyrians as Istar, to the Greeks as Aphrodite, and to the Romans as Venus. Since she was thought to control life and fertility in the area, worshipers adopted extreme measures to secure her favor. Through their own sexual relations at the altar of Baal and those of priests and priestesses, the people sought to encourage Baal and Ashtoreth to mate so as to fertilize the land, the animals, and the people. To ensure her fertility in marriage, a young lady would sit in the gate of the Baal shrine for seven days to engage in prostitution with the priests and/or strangers. The worship of Milcom, known also as Moleck, added the abominable act of child sacrifice—usually the firstborn—to their animal sacrifices and sensuous rites. Chemosh, the god of the Moabites, was also worshiped by the sacrifice of children as burnt offerings (2 Kings. 3:27). Solomon compounded his sin by erecting high places on the Mount of Olives for the worship of the abominable gods Chemosh and Molech (v. 7).

No wonder God was angry with Solomon (vv. 9-10). At least three times, God warned Solomon about his sin. He spoke with him—perhaps through a prophet—at the time of Solomon's building the house of God (6:11-13). He twice personally appeared to Solomon to keep him in the way, first at the beginning of Solomon's reign (3:5) and second in the twentieth year of Solomon's reign after he had completed the Temple and his palace (9:1-9).

Solomon's sin would result in the kingdom being taken from Solomon and given to his servant (v. 11). However, God would reserve "one tribe" for Solomon's son in order to fulfill his promise to David that David would always have a son on the throne in Jerusalem which God had chosen as the place where he was to be worshiped (v. 13). Also, for the sake of David, God would not take away the ten tribes until after the death of Solomon. Rehoboam, Solomon's son, would lose the kingdom. (v. 12). The "one tribe" (v. 13) probably refers to Judah, which absorbed Benjamin.

The adversaries God raised up are not to be taken as coming after the announcement of and as a mere punishment for Solomon's sin. These adversaries—Hadad the Edomite (vv. 14-22), Rezon the son of Eliada (vv. 23-25), and Jeroboam the son of Nebat (vv. 26-40)—were "the rod of men . . . the stripes of the sons of men" God promised David to send upon his son Solomon when he committed iniquity (2 Sam. 7:14-15). Accordingly, these adversaries were emissaries of God's steadfast love intended to lead Solomon back into the true worship of God. Solomon, however, "clung" (v. 2) to his foreign wives and indolatrous practices in spite of God's chastening hand.

Jeroboam's rebellion against Solomon resulted from Ahijah's dramatic prophecy that God would take the ten tribes of Northern Israel from Solomon and that Jeroboam would rule over these tribes (vv. 29-37). God gave Jeroboam a conditional promise in announcing that he would make him king over the ten tribes (vv. 38-39). The condition was whole-hearted obedience to God on the part of Jeroboam (v. 38a). His promises were: (1) to be with Jeroboam (v. 38b); (2) to build him a sure house as he built for David (v. 38c); and (3) to give to Jeroboam the ten tribes of Israel (v. 38d). "And I will for this afflict the descendants of David" (v. 39a) means that God would restrict the descendants of David to the kingdom of Judah because of the sin of Solomon and also to fulfill God's promise to Jeroboam. "But not forever" (v. 39b) means that God would not fail to fulfill his glorious promise to David ultimately to establish his throne forever over all Israel. In Christ, God's commitment to David will be completely fulfilled. Solomon sought to put Jeroboam to death upon learning of the prophecy, but Jeroboam escaped to Egypt (v. 40).

Summary of Solomon's Reign and His Death (11:41-43)

"The book of the acts of Solomon" was a book in which more information could be found concerning all that Solomon did. Solomon, who began reigning at the age of approximately twenty, died at about sixty years of age. His sin also attributed to the shortening of his life (3:14). Solomon loved God as a young man (2 Sam. 7:14-15; 1 Kings 3:3). However, we do not know whether he turned back to God from the pronounced sin of his old age. If Solomon wrote Ecclesiastes, we find hope there that in the end Solomon turned from his sins to fear the Lord and to keep his commandments (Eccl. 12:13-14).

The Division of the Kingdom (12:1-24)

At the death of Solomon, the United Hebrew Kingdom was divided as God promised. The Northern and Southern Kingdoms had been solidified under David and continued under Solomon (2 Sam. 2:4; 5:3; 1 Chron. 29:22-25). The union seemed, however, always to be tenuous because of the jealousy between Ephraim and Judah, the major tribes. Rehoboam had to be accepted by both the southern and northern tribes to be king over all Israel. Judah and Benjamin did make Rehoboam Solomon's successor. But the ten tribes rejected him and established Jeroboam for their king. This section recounts Rehoboam's journey to Shechem to be made king of all Israel (v. 1), the request of the ten tribes led by Jeroboam the son of Nebat for relief from heavy burdens imposed by Solomon (vv. 2-4), Rehoboam's consultations concerning the request (vv. 5-11), Rehoboam's decision to impose greater burdens on the people (vv. 12-15), the revolt of the ten tribes and the establishment of the kingdom of Israel with Jeroboam as king (vv. 16-20), and God's word forbidding Rehoboam's fighting to restore the ten tribes (vv. 21-24).

The Divided Kingdoms of Judah and Israel to the End of Israel
1 Kings 12:25 to 2 Kings 17:41

These chapters trace the history of the divided kingdoms of Judah and Israel until the fall of Israel, at which time Judah stood alone. Israel never had a king that did right in the sight of God and never experienced a revival of true religion. In contrast, many kings of Judah were devoted to the Lord God of Israel, if not with a perfect heart. Moreover, Judah experienced from time to time revivals by which the people were brought back to God. The focus in these chapters is on the taking of the kingdom from the house of Jeroboam (1 Kings 13:34; 14:10-11; 15:28-30), from the house of Baasha (1 Kings 16:7,11-13), from the house of Omri/Ahab (2 Kings 9:14 to 10:27), and from the house of Jehu (2 Kings 10:30; 15:12). Interspersed between the house of Baasha and the house of Ahab was the seven day reign of Zimri (1 Kings 16:15-20). After the fall of the house of Jehu, five kings of Israel came in rapid succession, without any being able to establish a dynasty. In contrast, God maintained throughout these turbulent years a son of David on the throne of Judah in faithfulness to his promise and often in spite of the wickedness of that king.

The Reign of Jeroboam of Israel (12:25 to 14:20)

This section recounts Jeroboam's fortification of Shechem and Penuel as defense cities (12:25), his sin of golden calf worship (12:26-33), the prophecy by the man of God against the golden calf altar at Bethel (13:1-10), the seduction of the man of God by the old prophet (13:11-19), the punitive death of the man of God (13:20-32), Jeroboam's persistence in calf worship (13:33-34), the prophecy of Ahijah concerning the cutting off of Jeroboam's house and of the captivity of Israel (14:1-18). It concludes with a summary of Jeroboam's reign (14:19-20).

Jeroboam's Sin (12:25-33)

Jeroboam took two steps to solidify his kingdom immediately upon his becoming king of Israel. First, he fortified Shechem and Penuel into defense cities (12:25). Second, he provided a substitute religion. Jeroboam was afraid the people, because of their worship of the Lord in Jerusalem, would give their allegiance once again to the house of David and kill him (12:26-33). The two calves, which he set up in high places to the north in Dan and to the south in Bethel, were similar to the golden calf made by Aaron in the wilderness (Ex. 32:4). The calves were probably made of wood and overlaid with gold. The calves may have been intended as a substitute for the ark in Jerusalem as the throne of the invisible God. However, the words "Behold your gods, O Israel, who brought you up out of the land of Egypt" (v. 28) suggest that the calves were made as actual images of God himself. By placing these images in Dan and Bethel, he hoped to guarantee the presence and protection of God. "Calf" means a young bull, the symbol of strength and fertility.

The worship of bulls was a common practice in the ancient Near East. For example, the Canaanite god Baal was worshiped under the symbol of a bull and was pictured in Canaanite epics as mating with heifers to produce calves. The priests wore the masks of bulls, and the worship of Baal involved ritual prostitution by which Baal and his consort were encouraged to mate in the heavens so as to fertilize the soil, the vines, the animals, and so forth. Accordingly, calf worship involved idolatrous worship of the Lord with the licentious overtures of fertility religions such as Baalism.

To augment his new religion, Jeroboam committed other sins. He built shrines at the high places to house the calves (v. 31a), appointed priests from non-Levitical people to maintain the shrine (v. 31b), changed the time of the Feast of Tabernacles from the seventh to the eighth month, possibly to coincide with the later harvest of Northern Israel (v. 32), and usurped the power of the priesthood in his burning incense at Bethel to inaugurate the new worship (v. 33). Golden calf worship became known as "the sin(s) of Jeroboam" and was followed by every subsequent king of Israel (15:26,34; 16:7,26,31).

Prophecy, Seduction, and Death of the Man of God (13:1-32)

The mention of Josiah by name as the son of David who would destroy the calf altar in Bethel is thought by many to be an addition to the original text (v. 2). But God, who inspired the prediction, who verified the prophecy by miraculously causing the altar to be torn down and the ashes poured out, and who miraculously withered and healed the hand of Jeroboam, would have no trouble predicting Josiah by name more than three hundred years before the event.

The testing and punitive death of the man of God illustrates what could happen to any disciple of the Lord who does not obey the commission of God to the letter (vv. 11-25). The old prophet may have lied to the man of God out of envy or to boost his image by fellowship with a man of God who had such prophetic powers. Perhaps, the old prophet was not a true man of God. The experience of Balaam shows that an ungodly man can give a true prophecy (Num. 24:17-19; 2 Pet. 2:15). Normally, the lion would have eaten both the man and his donkey. The unnatural behavior of the lion and of the ass magnified the supernatural and showed that God caused his death as predicted by the old prophet (v. 22). God seemingly allowed the man of God to be tested and brought such severe punishment upon him for disobedience to show the necessity of trying the spirit to be sure it is of God and to show the horror of disobedience.

Jeroboam's Persistence in Calf Worship (13:33)

God's condemnation of calf worship should have led Jeroboam to repentance. However, he plunged deeper into the sin of calf worship by ordaining additional illegitimate people to the priesthood (v. 33).

Prophecy of Doom for the House of Jeroboam and of Israel; Death of Jeroboam (13:34 to 14:20)

Ahijah, the prophet who delivered God's conditional promise to Jeroboam, brought the message of condemnation of calf worship as the sin that would ultimately destroy both the house of Jeroboam and the nation of Israel. Jeroboam sent his wife in disguise to inquire of Ahijah concerning their sick child (14:1-4). Ahijah, told beforehand by God of her disguise and what he should say to her, delivered to her the message of doom (14:5-16). God would raise up a king over Israel who would destroy the house of Jeroboam (14:14). All of his sons and male servants would be put to death. Only the sick son, who would die the moment the mother reentered her city, would be buried in the grave (14:12-13). The rest would be devoured wherever they should fall—by dogs if they should fall in the city or by birds if they should fall in the fields (14:10-11). Moreover, God would root Northern Israel out of the Land and cast them into exile beyond the Euphrates (14:14-16). For the fulfillment of these prophecies, note 1 Kings 14:17-18; 1 Kings 15:29-30; 2 Kings 15:29; 17:23; 18:11.

The Reigns of Rehoboam, Abijam, and Asa of Judah (14:21 to 15:24)

The reigns of three kings of Judah are dealt with before returning in 15:25 to the reigns of the kings of the newly established kingdom of Israel.

The Reign of Rehoboam (14:21-31)

This section includes general observations concerning the reign of Solomon's son Rehoboam (vv. 21-24), the record of the pillage of the house of the Lord by Shishak of Egypt to punish Judah for their sin (vv. 25-28), and a summary of Rehoboam's reign (vv. 29-31). Rehoboam, who was strengthened politically and religiously by the migration of the Levites to Jerusalem from Northern Israel, followed at least superficially in the ways of the Lord for a period of about three years (2 Chron.

11:13-17). However, when he was firmly established as king, Rehoboam turned from God and led Judah to sin more "than their fathers had done" (v. 22). Rehoboam did from time-to-time continue to worship in the house of the Lord (v. 28). Their sin is described as doing "what was evil in the sight of the Lord" (v. 22). "Evil" is "the evil" (note "all the abominations"—v. 24) and denotes those self-corrupting sins of the Canaanites' fertility cults by which they polluted themselves, defiled their land, and caused their expulsion from the land. "Pillars" (v. 23) were stone monuments and/or images erected in the high places to Baal. Some Baal images portrayed Baal in human form with the head of a bull. "Asherim" (v. 23) were wooden symbols of the fertility mother goddess Asherah, the consort of Baal. The "male cult prostitutes" (v. 24) were perhaps Canaanites who were imported for the purpose of teaching the Judahites "the fine art" of Baal worship, which involved unnatural sexual relations as well as natural abuses. Included also were female cult prostitutes who participated in the licentious acts by which Baal was encouraged to mate with Asherah to induce productivity of the land, the herds, and human families.

The punishment God promised to send upon his disobedient people was not slow in coming. Shishak the king of Egypt invaded Judah in the fifth year of Rehoboam's reign (v. 25). Shishak left on the wall of the great temple of Karnak in Egypt the record of this invasion. According to that record, Shishak conquered cities in both Judah and Israel. Jerusalem itself was saved only when the princes of Judah and Rehoboam humbled themselves before the Lord at the word of Shemaiah the prophet (2 Chron. 12:5-8). However, God allowed Shishak to take away all of the treasures of the house of God and all of the treasures of the king's house, including the shields of gold (v. 26). Accordingly, the glory of Solomon's kingdom and the house he built for God did not last long because of his and his son's sin against the Lord.

God's punishment of Judah is said to be rooted in his "jealousy" (v. 22). "Jealousy" describes the color in the face produced by intense anger, as though a person were dyed with red dye. Just as the husband desires the complete love of his wife and burns in wrath against any rival, so God poured out his wrath upon his people to destroy their sin that separated them from him.

The Reign of Abijam (15:1-8)

Abijam, the son and successor of Rehoboam, is also called Abijah (2 Chron. 13:1). "Abijah" means "Jehovah is my father," and he did show some respect for the Lord in bringing freewill gifts to the house of the Lord and in calling on him to give victory in battle (2 Chron. 13:4-18). However, Abijam, which means "my father is Yam" (a Canaanite god of the sea) more aptly describes his way. His heart was not true to the Lord. He followed Canaanite fertility practices as did Rehoboam, his earthly father (v. 3). Accordingly, religious apostasy deepened under Abijam and only God's steadfast love toward David kept God from removing Abijam from the throne and destroying Jerusalem and the people (vv. 4-5). Abijam was taught to be an extension of Rehoboam, so that reference could be made to the warfare between Rehoboam and Jeroboam that continued throughout the reign of Abijam (v. 6). Abijam's victory was extensive, inasmuch as he broke the powers of Jeroboam and took many of his cities (2 Chron. 13:18-20).

The Reign of Asa (15:9-24)

This section contains general observations concerning Asa's reign (vv. 9-10), his devotion to God and to the house of God (vv. 11-15), his war with Baasha king of Israel and alliance with Ben-hadad king of Syria (vv. 16-22), and a summary of his reign (vv. 23-24). Fortunate for the survival of Judah, the wicked but comparatively short reigns of Rehoboam and of Abijam were followed by the good and long reign of Asa (vv. 9-11). Maacah was actually the mother of Abijam and the grandmother of Asa (vv. 2,10). However, perhaps due to the death of Asa's mother, she continued in the highly influential role of queen mother during the early reign of Asa.

Asa turned Judah back to the worship of the Lord through his personal godliness and religious reforms. Apparently, there were two stages to Asa's religious reforms, the first being at the time of his beginning to reign and the second beginning about his fifteenth year as king (2 Chron. 14:2-6; 15:8-15).

Among his steps to promote the true worship of God were: (1) his removal out of the land of the male cult prostitutes that had been brought in by his father (v. 12a); (2) his removal of the pillars of Baal and images of Asherah that his father had set up in the high places (v. 12b); (3) his removal of Maacah as queen mother, because she was a chief devotee of Asherah (v. 13a); (4) his destruction of the queen mother's image of Asherah (v. 13b); (5) his beginning to replenish the treasury of the house of the Lord that had been pillaged by Shishak of Egypt (v. 15); (6) his repair of the great altar of sacrifice that was in front of the vestibule of the house of the Lord (2 Chron. 15:8); and (7) his gathering all of the people at the house of God in Jerusalem to worship the Lord (2 Chron. 15:10). Apparently, he also took away the altars and the high places his father had erected to the Canaanite gods (2 Chron. 14:3,5). The "high places" he failed to root out (v. 14a) were probably the country shrines after the manner of Canaanite altars that were used for the worship of the Lord. These were not removed until the reforms of Josiah (2 Kings 23:4-20). The notation that Asa was "wholly true to the Lord all his days" (v. 14b) probably indicates that these country shrines remained in spite of his effort to purify the worship of the Lord and to centralize it in Jerusalem. Many of Asa's reforms were inspired by the influence of the prophet Azariah the son of Oded (2 Chron. 15:1-8).

The Book of 2 Chronicles, which is based at least in part on "the Book of the Chronicles of the Kings of Judah" (v. 23), gives extensive treatment to the reign of Asa. There several deviations of Asa from perfect faith in the Lord are described. One was his making an alliance with Ben-hadad of Syria for protection against Baasha of Israel instead of trusting in God for protection as he had done in the case of the Ethiopian invasion (2 Chron. 16:7-9). Another was his punishment of Hanani the seer and his supporters when Hanani rebuked him for turning for help to Ben-hadad instead of to the Lord's (2 Chron. 16:10). A final deviation was in his old age in relation to his foot disease (v. 23). Instead of seeking the help of the Lord, he sought only the help of physicians and died (2 Chron. 16:12-13).

The Reign of Nadab: The End of the House of Jeroboam (15:25-32)

The forty-one year reign of Asa overlapped the reigns of kings of Israel from Jeroboam to Ahab. The most significant thing about the reign of Nadab the son of Jeroboam is the destruction of the house of Jeroboam by Baasha in fulfillment of the prophecy of Ahijah the Shilonite (14:7-11). Baasha assassinated Nadab at Gibbethon where Nadab and his army were in siege of that Philistine city (vv. 27-28). Then Baasha killed all of the males and perhaps every person of the house of Jeroboam (v. 29). Note especially the care given to show that the house of Jeroboam was destroyed because of the golden calf worship by which Jeroboam himself sinned, made the northern tribes to sin, and provoked the wrath of God (v. 30). No record is given of the dogs and the birds eating the bodies of the slain members of Jeroboam's house.

The Reigns of Baasha and of Elah His Son: The End of the House of Baasha (15:33 to 16:14)

The house of Baasha was short-lived. Baasha reigned for twenty-four years (15:33). He was succeeded by his son Elah, who reigned only two years before he was assassinated and succeeded by Zimri, one of his military commanders. Zimri destroyed the total house of Baasha (16:8-13). Jehu the son of Hanani predicted the destruction of Baasha's house (16:1-4). He gave two reasons for which God would destroy Baasha's house: (1) because Baasha and Elah walked in the same evil ways of calf worship as the house of Jeroboam whom they replaced (vv. 2b,7a,13); and (2) because of the way Baasha destroyed the house of Jeroboam (v. 7b). God raised up Baasha to destroy the house of Jeroboam; however, God did not approve of the manner in which Baasha executed the punishment. Baasha's relish and violence in shedding their blood must have been involved. Jehu implied in his message of doom that Baasha and his house should have served the Lord in gratitude for his exalting them from their lowly position to rule over Israel (v. 2a). The devouring dogs and birds again symbolize the violent death of the male heirs of the house of Baasha. In his execution of judgment, Zimri went beyond the male heirs to the throne and put to death also every male "of his kinsmen or his friends" (v. 11). "Kinsmen" refers to any blood relation who might seek to avenge Baasha's death.

The Reign of Zimri (16:15-20)

Zimri lasted only seven days as king of Israel (v. 15a). As soon as the military leaders and their troops heard of Zimri's assassination of the house of Baasha and his establishment of himself as king, they proclaimed Omri, the commander of the army, king (vv. 15b-16). Omri immediately besieged Zimri in Tirzah (v. 17). When Zimri saw that Tirzah was taken, he went to the citadel of the king's house and committed suicide by burning the house over his head (v. 18). His failure to be established as king and his death were also due to his following and influencing others to follow in the evil practices of calf worship (v. 19).

The Reign of Omri (16:21-28)

At the time of Omri's being made king by the military, the people were divided in their loyalties between him and Tibni the son of Ginath (v.

21). However, Omri established himself as king of all Israel after four years of struggle. The newly established house of Omri, often called "the house of Ahab" after Omri's most famous son, lasted for forty-eight years—through the reigns of Omri, Ahab, Ahaziah, and Jehoram. After reigning for six of his twelve years at Tirzah, Omri bought a hill from Shemer for the small sum of two talents of silver, fortified it, and made it his capital city. The hill guarded the fertile valley in the midst of which it stood. The valley itself was surrounded by mountains. Ahab named the hill "Samaria," meaning "place of watch," after Shemer, since his name expressed the ideas of guarding and keeping. Samaria was the capital of Northern Israel from that time until its destruction by the Assyrians in 722 BC (2 Kings 18:8-10). Omri also followed the evil practices of calf worship instituted by Jeroboam (v. 26). However, he was worse than any king before him in the pursuit of wickedness (v. 25).

The Reign of Ahab (16:29 to 22:40)

Ahab's reign was the most significant in the history of Northern Israel from a religious point of view. The main reason is the crisis that occurred in his reign between the true worshipers of the Lord and those who debased the worship of the Lord or would substitute some other god for the Lord God of Israel. The prophets of Israel, led by Elijah and Elisha, championed the worship of the Lord and him only in the purity of the laws of Moses. The struggle resulted in the destruction of the house of Omri and the purging of Baalism from Israel. However, the sin of Jeroboam, which would lead ultimately to the destruction of the nation, continued to flourish.

The Beginning of His Reign (16:29-34)

After a brief statement dating the reign of Ahab (v. 29), this passage concentrates on the sin of Ahab (vv. 30-33) and notes the fulfillment of Joshua's prophecy concerning the curse of rebuilding Jericho (v. 34). Like his father Omri, Ahab was undaunted by God's judgment upon other wicked kings and their houses. He plunged deeper into wickedness than any who reigned before him (v. 30). He not only perpetuated the evil practices of calf worship (v. 31a), but pressed Baal worship upon Israel (vv. 31b-33). Ahab took for his queen Jezebel, the daughter of Ethbaal the king of Sidon. Ethbaal was also a priest of Baal, who was worshiped among the Sidonians under the name Baal-Melkart. Jezebel herself was an ardent devotee of Baal and zealously sought to make Baalism the religion of Israel. Ahab continued to name allegiance to the Lord God of Israel as is reflected by his giving his children Yahweh names: Ahaz-*iah*, *Jeh*-oram, and Athal-*iah*. However, Ahab himself became a worshiper of Baal (v. 31*b*). He built in Samaria a house devoted to the worship of Baal (v. 32), erected in it an altar to Baal (v. 32), built an image to Asherah the female consort of Baal (v. 33*a*), and erected a pillar to Baal (2 Kings 3:2). Also, Ahab gave Jezebel free rein to press her desire to make the people of Israel worshipers of Baal. To that end, she sought to wipe out the prophets of the Lord God of Israel (18:4) and appointed and maintained a large number of priests and priestesses of Baal and Asherah to practice and teach that abominable worship (18:19). The wicked influence of Jezebel and Ahab also devastated Judah. Their daughter Athaliah, who married Jehoram king of Judah, extended the abominable influence of Baalism in Judah (2 Kings 8:18) and all but destroyed the royal lineage of David (2 Kings 11:1-3). Ahab's reign is summed up in saying that he did more "to provoke the Lord, the God of Israel, to anger than all the kings of Israel who were before him" (v. 33*b*). "Whom Jezebel his wife incited" is added to a later but similar description of his wickedness (21:25).

The record of the violation of Joshua's command not to rebuild Jericho into a fortified city under penalty of a curse is included to illustrate the depth of their wickedness (v. 34; Josh. 6:26). Hiel lived in Bethel under the tragic influence of golden calf worship. Violation of one command led to violation, neglect, and/or ignorance of others. But Hiel paid for his violation or ignorance with the deaths of Abiram his first-born son and of Segub his youngest son. Abiram and Segub were perhaps killed on the job, as they were involved respectively in laying the foundation and in setting up the gates of the fortified city.

Ahab and Elijah (17:1 to 19:21)

During that time of religious and national crisis, the Lord God of Israel raised up Elijah the Tishbite, one of the most powerful of all his prophets. Certainly, Elijah stood in line with Moses and Samuel as the greatest leaders of the true worship of the Lord. Elijah served in the Northern Kingdom during the reigns of Ahab and his son Ahaziah. This section recounts: the miraculous drought and feeding of Elijah (17:1-24); the contest of gods on Mount Carmel (18:1-40); the miraculous end of the drought (18:41-46); the wrath of Jezebel toward Elijah (19:1-2); Elijah's fear, flight, and despair (19:3-8); Elijah's reassurance and commission (19:9-18); and Elijah's call of Elisha to be prophet in his place (19:19-21).

The miraculous drought and feeding of Elijah (17:1-24).—Not a great deal is known about Elijah. He is here spoken of as "Elijah the Tishbite, of Tishbe in Gilead" (17:1). "Elijah" means "the Lord is my God." He was from Gilead, which was located on the eastern side of the Jordan River. He was a member of the family and/or town called "Tishbe," from whence he was called "the Tishbite." Elsewhere, we learn that he customarily wore a garment of "haircloth," most likely of skin or of coarse camel's hair, with a girdle or belt of leather about his waist (2 Kings 1:8). Apparently, he appeared and disappeared quite suddenly as if carried to and fro by the Spirit of God (18:12). He was associated with and perhaps was the head of the school of prophets, which had been started by Samuel the prophet (1 Sam. 19:20; 2 Kings 2:7,16-18). His great physical endurance is illustrated by his running before Ahab's chariot from Mount Carmel to the entrance of the city of Jezreel, a distance of not less than fifteen miles (1 Kings 18:46). His devotion to God caused him to have great concern for the nation of Israel and great boldness in calling the leaders and people of Israel to wholehearted devotion to the Lord God of Israel alone. God gave Elijah the power of miracles to authenticate his ministry and to prove the superiority of the Lord God of Israel to any so-called god.

True to his mystique, Elijah appeared suddenly and dramatically on the scene to announce to Ahab in the name of the Lord God of Israel that there would be neither dew nor rain for the next years except at the word of Elijah (17:1). The miraculous drought and feeding of Elijah struck at the heart of Baalism, especially the worship of Baal-Melkart of the Sidonians, whom Jezebel and Ahab had enthroned in Israel in the place of the Lord God of Israel. Baal-Melkart was supposed to provide the rain and other ingredients necessary to produce life and fertility in the Land. The actual drought, which seemingly engulfed Sidon as well as all of the Northern Kingdom, proved the power of the Lord God of Israel and the impotence of Baal. God's miraculous feeding of Elijah by the ravens (vv. 2-7) and by the widow of Zarephath (vv. 8-16) illustrated God's ability and commitment to care for his own even in Zarephath, which was the home territory of Baal-Melkart. The miraculous multiplication of the meal and the oil when the widow obeyed Elijah's command to feed him first demonstrated how God would provide for those who put him first in their lives. The widow interpreted the death of her son as punishment from God for her sin (v. 18). She supposed that the punishment had come upon her sin because the holy God who will tolerate no evil was brought near to her in the person of Elijah. Elijah interpreted the death of the son to be another of the calamities that God had caused to come on Israel and Sidon to demonstrate that he alone is God (v. 20). The purpose of Elijah's stretching himself three times on the son is not known. Some say that he sought to transfer his vitality into the dead body. In any case, the miraculous living again of the son in response to Elijah's prayer demonstrated that God has the power to restore life (vv. 21-23). The miracle caused the woman to know for sure that Elijah was a man of God and that the Lord God of Israel in whose name Elijah spoke is the true God (v. 24).

The contest of gods on Mount Carmel (18:1-40).—After three years of drought, God commanded Elijah to return to Israel for a contest between the Lord God of Israel and Baal to determine once for all who should be the God of Israel. We are first told of Elijah's confrontation of Ahab demanding the test of gods (vv. 1-19) and then of the trial by fire on Mount Carmel by which the Lord God of Israel demonstrated himself alone to be God (vv. 20-40). The severity in Samaria of the drought and resultant famine is illustrated by Ahab's and Obadiah's search for water and grass to save the lives of the animals (vv. 2b-6). Elijah, charged by Ahab with being the "troubler of Israel," pointed out that the root of Israel's problem for which God had sent the drought as chastisement was the sin of Ahab and his father's house (vv. 17-18). Every king of the Northern Kingdom had walked in the evil practices of calf worship introduced by Jeroboam. However, Ahab's father Omri had plunged deeper into the wickedness of this sin than any king before him (16:25). Moreover, Ahab continued the evil practice of his father and added the sin of pushing on Israel the worship of Baalism (16:30-33).

Ahab gathered together at Mount Carmel the people of Israel and the prophets of Baal in response to Elijah's challenge for a contest of gods (v. 20). Omission of any further reference to the priestesses suggests that they did not officially take part, but left the test to the priests. Elijah challenged the people to decide by the test of fire who is the true God and then to follow him with all their hearts (vv. 21-24). The prophets of Baal failed to get any response from Baal (vv. 25-29), but the Lord answered by fire in response to Elijah's prayer (vv. 36-38). The twelve stones were used to demonstrate that the division of the nation into two kingdoms was due to sin and that truly repairing God's altar in their hearts would restore the union of the nation. The pouring of water on the sacrifice was most likely to make the sacrifice more difficult and to remove any possible deception. "The fire of the Lord" was supernatural fire, associated with the presence of God (Lev. 9:24; 1 Chron. 21:26). The miracle convinced the people that the Lord God of Israel alone is the one true

God, and they reverently committed themselves to follow him (v. 39). The slaughter of the prophets of Baal carried out God's command to destroy false prophets (Deut. 17:2-7).

The miraculous end of the drought (18:41-46).—The larger issue in the contests of gods was to determine who could bring rain. The Lord God of Israel at the word of Elijah sent a great rain to end the drought in response to the return of the people to him. Elijah's command to Ahab to go down immediately "lest the rain stop you" (v. 44) was to cross the valley before the Kishon was flooded by the great rain.

Elijah's fear, flight, and despair (19:1-8).—The victory at Mount Carmel was a crucial battle in the war with Baalism. However, the final victory did not come until much later in the days of Elisha when Jehu purged Baalism from the land (2 Kings 10:18-28). Elijah's joy was turned to fear, flight, and despair by the wrath of Jezebel, who vowed to kill him just as he had killed the prophets of Baal (v. 2). Elijah fled first to Beersheba, which was far south in the kingdom of Judah. There seeking solitude, he went a day's journey into the desert to pour out to God his weariness with the struggle to establish his people in true covenant relation with the Lord and his request to die. In referring to his "fathers" (v. 4), Elijah suggested that he was already the age when death would be normal. God, however, still had a great work for Elijah to do. Accordingly, God brought Elijah in the strength of supernatural care to Mount Horeb, where he reassured Elijah and commissioned him to further work.

Elijah's reassurance and commission (19:9-18).—"A cave" (v. 9) is "the cave." Reference is probably to the cleft in the rock where God covered Moses with his hand while he passed by in all his glory (Ex. 33:21-23). The meaning of God's revelation of himself seems to be that God would not punish Israel and destroy Baalism by spectacular methods such as tornado, earthquake, and/or fire, but by the seemingly quiet course of daily life (19:11-17). Accordingly, God would avenge himself by the providentially controlled ministries of Hazael, king of Syria, Jehu, king of Israel, and of Elisha, the prophet, all of whom Elijah was to appoint to their respective offices. The righteous remnant of seven thousand were those true to God in Elijah's day whom God would use to build the future glory of Israel (v. 18).

The call of Elisha to be prophet in Elijah's place (19:19-21).—Elijah returned to the Northern Kingdom and called Elisha to be prophet in his place. The anointing of Hazael and Jehu occurred later and was accomplished through Elisha in the case of Hazael (2 Kings 8:13) and through

an unnamed prophet sent by Elisha in the case of Jehu (2 Kings 9:1-10).
The twelve yoke of oxen probably indicate that Shaphat, Elisha's father,
was a wealthy farmer. The mantle was the upper garment worn for
warmth by both men and women. Elijah's mantle was probably of a
special character—most likely of animal hair—to designate the prophetic office. In placing his mantle on Elisha, Elijah symbolically
claimed him to be his successor. Elisha accepted the call and after a fare-
well feast with his family and friends followed Elijah. The later comment that Elisha "poured water on the hands of Elijah" (2 Kings 3:11)
probably indicates that he rendered special service to Elijah during those
early days. Elisha is not heard from again until prior to Elijah's translation (2 Kings 2:1).

Ahab's Two Miraculous Victories Over Ben-hadad of Syria (20:1-43)

The story of Elijah and Ahab continues in chapter 21, but we turn
aside now to look at two miraculous victories God gave Ahab over the
Syrians in order to lead Ahab to recognize and serve him as the one true
God (vv. 13,18). War between Syria and the Northern Kingdom was
almost continuous during those days. Ben-hadad, whose father (also
called Ben-hadad) had conquered several cities of Galilee in the reigns of
Baasha and of Omri (15:20; 20:34), came with a great army and besieged the city of Samaria (v. 1). The "thirty-two kings" (v. 1) over the
army of Ben-hadad were rulers of various city-states of the Syrian kingdom of Ben-hadad. "The elders of the land" (v. 7) and "the governors of
the districts" (v. 14) had probably fled for refuge into the city of Samaria
before the face of the invading Syrians. Ahab yielded to Ben-hadad's first
demand, which Ahab interpreted to mean paying tribute as a vassal nation, but rebelled at the idea of unconditional surrender in the second
demand of Ben-hadad (vv. 2-9). By "the dust of Samaria shall suffice for
handfuls" (v. 10), Ben-hadad meant that he would reduce Samaria to a
small pile of ashes that his army could carry off in their hands. An unnamed prophet both predicted and guided Ahab in the first victory (vv.
13-21). Then the prophet instructed Ahab to prepare for Ben-hadad's
assault next spring (v. 22). An insight into the ancient Near Eastern
understanding of God is seen in the opinion of the Syrians that the god
of the Hebrews was a mountain god who could easily be defeated in the
plains (vv. 23-25). The Lord God of Israel showed himself to be the God
of universal power in destroying their army also in the plain (vv.
26-30a).

Ahab, however, failed to learn to obey the Lord God of Israel, as is indicated in his covenanting with Ben-hadad instead of putting him to death as God had decreed (vv. 35-43). "A certain man of the sons of the prophets" (v. 35) received instructions from the Lord to announce to Ahab that Ahab and his people would die for letting Ben-hadad and the Syrians go free (v. 42).

"The sons of the prophets" (v. 35) seem to refer to members of a guild of true prophets, whose lives were bound together in utter devotion to the Lord God of Israel and the proclamation of his word. "Son" probably carries the double idea of being spiritually begotten by the prophets and of being like them in character and ministry. These prophets flourished in spite of Jezebel's attempt to stamp them out (18:4,13). The majority seemingly dwelt together in some kind of communal living (2 Kings 4:38; 6:1). However, some were married and had their own private property and debts (2 Kings 4:1-3). Others lived apparently in other places throughout Israel (2 Kings 2:1-8; 5:22). This prophetic group is first heard of in the days of Samuel, who was perhaps both founder and head of the group (1 Sam. 19:20). Elijah was associated with them and perhaps also their head (2 Kings 2:3,5,7). Elisha, Elijah's successor, definitely served as their head (2 Kings 6:1). The definite article is added to prophets in the Hebrew expression translated "the sons of the prophets" (v. 35) to distinguish these true prophets from false prophets such as the prophets of Baal (1 Kings 18:19) and the court prophets (1 Kings 22:6). Amos did not disavow "the sons of the prophets" in declaring himself neither to have been a prophet nor the son of a prophet, but merely emphasized that he had no prior association with the prophetic ministry before God called him to prophesy (Amos 7:14).

The dramatic fashion in which the prophet delivered to Ahab the message of doom is quite in keeping with their methods. The devouring by the lion of the fellow prophet who failed to strike him "at the command of the Lord" (v. 35) served to warn all of severe punishment of those who disobey the word of God as it came through the prophet (v. 36). In the prophetic drama, the prophet posed as a warrior. He wanted to be struck and wounded to illustrate the suffering of Ahab and Israel at the hands of Ben-hadad. The man placed in his custody was a very valuable prisoner of war. The implied appeal of the wounded soldier was for Ahab, the commander of the army, to overturn the penalty for his neglect leveled by his superior. Ahab, however, refused to relieve the punishment, which had been agreed upon at his taking charge of the prisoner.

In like manner, God had placed Ben-hadad and the Syrians in the hands of Ahab and had decreed their death. "Devoted to destruction" (v.

42) translates the Hebrew word *cherem*, which in the basic sense means "to shut up or in." It is used of that which is exclusively devoted to the Lord and, thus, excluded from any other use. That which is devoted to the Lord may be either marked by the Lord for destruction, as in the case of Ben-hadad, or consecrated to the Lord for his exclusive use, as in the case of Jericho's treasures (Josh. 6:17-19). To take that which was devoted to the Lord, as in the case of Achan (Josh. 7:1), to fail to execute the decree of destruction placed upon it, as in the case of Ahab, or in any other way to violate the ban, would result in the violator himself and all that belonged to him being devoted irrevocably to the Lord for destruction. The severe penalty was due to the nature of the crime. *Cherem* was "most holy to the Lord" (Lev. 27:28). One who willfully violated that which was "most holy to the Lord" had committed the height of abomination. Accordingly, the prophet announced to Ahab that he and his people would die for allowing Ben-hadad and his people to escape. Ahab's "people" (v. 42) probably refer to the Israelites who were smitten in the continued war with the Syrians that could have been prevented by Ahab's carrying out God's decree to put Ben-hadad and his army to death. Ahab personified the house of Omri, all of whom were destroyed (2 Kings 9:14 to 10:11). "Resentful and sullen" (v. 43) carries the deeper ideas of "rebellious and raging." The dwelling to which Ahab returned was most likely his palace in Jezreel. "Samaria" now stands for Northern Israel.

Ahab, Elijah, and Naboth's Vineyard (21:1-29)

Sometime after Ahab's condemnation by the prophet for his failing to execute God's wrath on Ben-hadad and the Syrians, Ahab desired to obtain for a vegetable garden the vineyard of Naboth that adjoined the king's palace in Jezreel (vv. 1-2a). He offered Naboth either money or a better vineyard in exchange for his vineyard (v. 2b). But the vineyard was Naboth's God-given family inheritance or allotment in the Land, and Naboth was bound by the law of God to keep it for the sake of past, present, and future family (Lev. 25:23-28; Num. 36:7-9). Accordingly, Naboth refused Ahab's offer (v. 3). In invoking the name of the Lord, Naboth indicated that he was a true worshiper of the Lord God of Israel, one of the seven thousand in Israel who had not bowed the knee to Baal. The story that follows in verses 4-29 reports on Ahab's vexation at Naboth's refusal to sell him his vineyard (v. 4), Jezebel's plot of Naboth's death to secure the vineyard for Ahab (vv. 5-10), Naboth's murder according to Jezebel's plot (vv. 11-14), Ahab's seizure of Naboth's vineyard

(vv. 15-16), Elijah's confrontation of and pronouncement of doom upon Ahab and his house (vv. 17-24), and Ahab's humiliation of himself before God and consequential postponement of the end of his house till the days of his son (vv. 27-29). Provided also is a parenthetic summary of Ahab's evil (vv. 25-26).

Although Ahab sulked like a child about the palace in Samaria (v. 4), he seemed willing to honor God's law of family inheritance. Jezebel, however, was enraged at Naboth's refusal and at Ahab's acceptance of the laws of the land (vv. 5-7). She then orchestrated the death of Naboth and Ahab's possession of the vineyard. "The elders and the nobles" (v. 8) to whom she sent the letters ordering Naboth's death were the judges of Jezreel who were responsible for enacting justice (Deut. 16:28). Their joining Jezebel in the plot to kill Naboth and steal his vineyard shows the depth of moral corruption to which the nation as a whole had sunk and the great fear that the people had of Jezebel, the ruthless queen. The "fast" (v. 9) was a solemn assembly called because some terrible wrong had been done that was causing trouble in the Land. The high place given to Naboth was a place of honor (v. 9). However, "two base fellows," who would swear to anything for money, were placed opposite him to testify at the appropriate time. They said, "You have cursed God and the king" (v. 10). Naboth, thus, was charged with committing the evil that had caused the trouble in the Land. His sin, which was punishable by stoning to death (Lev. 24:16), could be removed only by his execution. We learn later from Jehu, who accompanied Ahab from Samaria to Jezreel to possess the vineyard, that Naboth's sons were also put to death, so that there was no heir to contest Ahab's possession of the land (2 Kings 9:26).

The word of the Lord came to Elijah commanding him to confront Ahab with his evil and to pronounce the doom of Ahab and his house. Both Elijah and Ahab could be spoken of as going "down" to Jezreel because they came respectively from the heights of Mount Carmel and Samaria (vv. 16,18). Elijah, who appeared once again suddenly and unexpectedly, caught Ahab red-handed. "Have you killed" (v. 19) shows that God laid the responsibility of Naboth's murder at Ahab's feet. Although Jezebel did the work in his name, Ahab consented to the evil deeds of murder and theft.

The condemnation of Ahab and his house was fourfold. First, Ahab would die for taking the life of Naboth. Indeed, the dogs would lick Ahab's blood "in the place" (v. 19) where dogs licked up the blood of Naboth. "In the place" probably was not intended to designate the exact spot, inasmuch as Naboth was stoned to death outside the city of Jezreel and the dogs licked Ahab's blood at the pool of Samaria where the chariot that bore Ahab's body was washed (22:38). However, the bloody bodies of Naboth and his sons may have been carried for burial in some vehicle—official or otherwise—that was later washed at the pool of Samaria where the dogs licked their blood. Second, the house of Ahab would be totally destroyed as God destroyed the house of Jeroboam and the house of Baasha (vv. 21-22). Every male of his house, whether his son or servant, would be put to death. Third, the dogs would eat Jezebel within the city of Jezreel (v. 23). Fourth, all belonging to Ahab would die a violent death (v. 24). Those who died in the city would be eaten by dogs and those who died in the open country would be eaten by the birds of the air. "Incited" (v. 25) means that Jezebel was the instigator of Ahab in the evil for which he, Jezebel, and his house would be violently cut off.

God's pronouncement of judgment on Ahab by Elijah caused Ahab to humble himself before God (v. 27). Whether Ahab truly repented so that he was forgiven and experienced all the blessings implied in our word "salvation," we do not know. God did, however, moderate his judgment concerning the destruction of the house of Ahab (vv. 28-29). That destruction would now take place after the death of Ahab "in his son's days." Ahab had two sons, Ahaziah and Jehoram, who reigned respectively for two years and twelve years. His house was cut off in the days of Jehoram (2 Kings 9:14 to 10:17). (Jehoram and Joram are variant spellings of the same name, 2 Kings 3:1 and 2 Kings 9:14.)

Ahab's Continued War with Syria and His Death (22:1-40)

After a lapse of three years, the smoldering war between Syria and Israel flared up again (v. 1). This time Ahab himself instigated the conflict, seemingly because of Ben-hadad's failure to return as promised in the treaty the ancient Israelite city of Ramoth-gilead (v. 3). Ramoth-gilead, a border town, was located in the mountains of Gilead east of the Jordan River opposite Jezreel. Ramoth-gilead means "height of Gilead," and this city was strategic in controlling the eastern caravan route. This section deals with: Ahab's alliance with Jehoshaphat of Judah for the war to retake Ramoth-gilead (vv. 2-4); Ahab and Jehoshaphat's inquiry of the prophets as to the word of God concerning the war (vv. 5-28); and the death of Ahab and the defeat of their combined armies according to prophecy (vv. 29-40).

The four hundred prophets assembled by Ahab were prophets of the Lord, as is indicated by Jehoshaphat's desire to hear "the word of the

Lord" (v. 5), by Jehoshaphat's referring to them as prophets of the Lord (v. 7), and by Zedekiah's claim to have been moved by "the Spirit of the Lord" (v. 24). However, in contrast with Micaiah the son of Imlah, they were not true prophets of the Lord. They are referred to in the heavenly council as Ahab's prophets (v. 22), which probably means that they depended on Ahab for their support and that they allowed themselves to be influenced by him. Many speak of them as "court prophets." Zedekiah's name means "the righteous of the Lord"; however, his use of the horns to dramatize the victory of Ahab and Jehoshaphat (v. 11) suggests that these prophets worshiped the Lord in accord with the sin of Jeroboam in making the golden calves. Some conjecture that Micaiah had the reputation with Ahab of being a doom prophet because Micaiah was the prophet who pronounced doom on Ahab, his house, and the people of Israel for Ahab's making the treaty with Ben-hadad instead of executing him as one "devoted to destruction" by the Lord (20:42).

Micaiah's first reply was a sarcastic repetition of the false message of the four hundred prophets (v. 15). However, in response to Ahab's plea, he delivered to him the word of God (vv. 16-17,19-23). Micaiah predicted Ahab's death in describing Israel "as sheep that have no shepherd" (v. 17a). By his picture of the defeated Israelites being allowed to return to their homes in peace (v. 17b), Micaiah predicted that the Syrians would make no attempt to destroy the army of Ahab at his death.

Micaiah explained the false messages of the four hundred prophets by his vision in which he saw "a lying spirit" (v. 22) go forth from the presence of God to deceive Ahab's prophets. The throne scene portrays God's sovereign control of everything, even evil spirits. God had decreed that Ahab should be brought to his just fate by death at Ramoth-gilead. The question of the council of heaven concerns what method should be used to bring it to pass. "A spirit" (v. 21) is "the spirit" in Hebrew and seems to personify the spirit of prophecy, which controlled the action of both true and false prophets (1 John 4:1-6). However, many identify "the spirit" (v. 21) with Satan, following the analogy of the heavenly council in Job 1:6-12. The method agreed on to bring about Ahab's death was to cause Ahab and his prophets to believe "a lying spirit" (v. 22). Ahab and his prophets themselves brought on and caused their susceptibility to this delusion by their following such wickedness as calf worship. In their turning the truth of God into a lie, they became futile in their thinking and darkened their minds (Rom. 1:21). Zedekiah illustrates the total delusion of these prophets, who had so seared their consciences that they actually thought themselves to be true prophets and that the Spirit of the

Lord had actually given to them the message of victory (v. 24). Micaiah told Zedekiah that Zedekiah would discover himself to be a false prophet at the time of his fleeing to his inner chamber seeking to escape the judgment of God (v. 25).

Ahab responded to Micaiah's prophecy by putting him in prison (v. 27). Ahab's delusion of victory is seen in his belief that he would return from the battle in peace (v. 27). With the words, "If you return in peace, the Lord has not spoken by me" (v. 28), Micaiah indicated that fulfillment of prophecy was one test to determine genuine prophets. Ahab took precautions in the ensuing battle by disguising himself. However, God struck Ahab down with an arrow shot at random by a bowman. The arrow struck Ahab in the stomach between the scale armor that covered the lower portion of his body and the breastplate, and he died in the evening (vv. 34-35). The blood of his wounds, which flowed into the bottom of the chariot, was washed out at the pool of Samaria (v. 38). There it was licked up by dogs as predicted by Elijah (21:19). The reference to the harlots (v. 38*b*), who apparently were washing themselves at the same time the chariot was washed, was not part of Elijah's prophecy. Their washing themselves with the water into which his blood ran shows that his desecrated blood was mingled in death with the harlotry he promoted by his wickedness. Archaeologists have identified in Samaria Ahab's "ivory house" (v. 39). The palace itself was of stone with paneling and furniture inlaid with ivory.

The Reign of Jehoshaphat of Judah (22:41-50)

Although good king Jehoshaphat reigned over Judah for twenty-five years, very little attention is given to his reign in the King's material. Contrast 2 Chronicles 17:1 to 21:1. Apart from the general introductory and concluding matters, attention is given briefly to his godliness (v. 43), to his making peace with the king of Israel (v. 44), to his administration of Edom through a deputy (v. 47), and to his ill-fated maritime venture (vv. 48-49).

The main contribution of Jehoshaphat was his continuing to press the religious reforms begun by Asa his father. Their combined reigns of sixty-six years swept back the floodtide of wickedness that engulfed the life of Judah from the evil reigns of Rehoboam and Abijam. "The high places" (v. 43) not removed were those dedicated, many from early times, to the worship of the Lord. Like his father Asa, he did not have the power or the will to abolish these places of worship, which stood in violation of the command for the Temple in Jerusalem alone to be the place of sacrifice. He was, however, able to exterminate the remnant of the male cult prostitutes who remained in Judah after Asa's purge of them (v. 46).

His biggest mistake was in making alliances with the kings of Israel. Jehoshaphat's twenty-five-year reign over Judah overlapped the reigns of three kings of Israel—of Ahab for eighteen years, of Ahab's son Ahaziah for two years, and of Jehoram (Joram) for five years. Prior to Jehoshaphat's reign, there was continual war between Judah and Israel. Jehoshaphat, however, made peace with Ahab (v. 44) and maintained it thereafter with Ahab's sons who reigned in his stead. His search for peace with Israel may have been commendable. However, as part of his peace plan, he made an unholy marriage alliance with wicked Ahab and Jezebel by which his son Jehoram married their daughter Athaliah (2 Kings 8:18). See comments on 2 Kings 8:16-24; 8:25-29; 11:1-3; and 2 Chronicles 24:17-18 for the tragic results of this unholy alliance.

The Reign of Ahaziah of Israel (22:51-53)

After this brief introduction of the reign of Ahaziah of Israel, the Book of 1 Kings is brought to a close. Ahaziah succeeded Ahab as king over Israel. Like Ahab and Jezebel, his wicked father and mother, Ahaziah provoked the wrath of God upon Israel by following both the evil practices of calf worship introduced by Jeroboam the son of Nebat and of Baalism proliferated in Israel by Jezebel.

The Reign of Ahaziah of Israel Continued (2 Kings 1:1-18)

This passage continues the reign of Ahaziah of Israel, which was interrupted at the end of 1 Kings 22:53 by the division of the Books of 1 and 2 Kings. The decision by the translators of the Hebrew as to where to divide the books apparently was quite arbitrary. After the beginning and characterization of Ahaziah's evil reign found in 1 Kings 22:51-53, this passage describes the rebellion of Moab against Israel which took place after Ahab's death (v. 1) and Elijah's condemnation of Ahaziah for seeking revelation from Baalzebub, the god of Ekron (vv. 2-17a). This passage concludes with a summary of Ahaziah's reign, noting particularly his death according to Elijah's prophecy and his succession by

Jehoram, his brother, since he had no sons (vv. 17b-18).

The rebellion of Moab was another phase of the judgment of God upon the house of Ahab (Omri) for their evil. David subjugated the Moabites (2 Sam. 8:12), and they continued as vassals to Israel when the kingdom was split. But at the death of Ahab, they successfully rebelled. The king of Moab's account of his rebellion is found in the Moabite Stone, one of the treasures of archaeology. Apparently, the defeat and death of Ahab at the battle of Ramoth-gilead weakened the power of Israel in the Transjordan area. Ahaziah himself could do nothing about their rebellion because of his grave illness. Additional information about the rebellion is found in a later report of Jehoram's ill-fated attempt once again to subjugate Moab to Israel (2 Kings 3:4-27).

Ahaziah's illness was caused by his fall through the latticework that adorned the upper chamber of his palace in Samaria (v. 2). The upper chamber was built on the roof to provide a place both secluded and cool. The latticework was to conceal the inside of the chamber from view, but to allow the cool breezes to flow through. "Baalzebub" (v. 2), which means "the lord of flies," was the name under which Baal was worshiped at Ekron, the Philistine city. As "the lord of flies," Baal was thought to be both the producer of flies and the defender of the people against this pest. Baalzebub may have had the reputation of unusual prophetic powers.

"The angel of the Lord" (v. 3) who sent Elijah to speak the word of death concerning Ahaziah was the special presence by whom God personally revealed himself. Perhaps, God himself appeared to Elijah because of the special nature of Ahaziah's sin in inquiring of Baalzebub. It implied that the Lord God of Israel was incapable of providing the needed revelation and that they, thus, must turn for help to Baal. The message of condemnation indicated that the Lord God of Israel not only knew the future of Ahaziah's injury, but would cause the injury to be fatal to the apostate king for his turning to Baalzebub (v. 4). His punishment was in accord with the law's requirement of death for those who held in contempt the Lord God of Israel (Lev. 24:16).

The morality of Elijah's calling fire from heaven to consume the two captains and their fifties has been questioned, especially in light of Jesus' rebuking his disciples for wanting to call down fire upon those Samaritans who rejected Christ (Luke 9:54-55). The fire, however, was supernatural and shows that God himself executed the punishment. Note that "the fire of God came down from heaven" (v. 12b). Perhaps, this was God's way of protecting Elijah from Ahaziah's desire to kill Elijah. Also,

God perhaps executed upon them the death penalty required by the law for their contempt of the Lord God of Israel (Lev. 24:16). Their insolence toward Elijah certainly shows that they shared Ahaziah's contempt for Elijah and for the God he represented (vv. 9,11). Accordingly, their fiery execution provided a much needed, though harsh demonstration of God's judgment upon those who hold him in contempt. In contrast, Elijah at the instructions of the angel of the Lord went with the third captain who humbly recognized the reality of the Lord God of Israel and the power of his prophet, Elijah (vv. 13-16).

The Ministry of Elisha (2:1 to 8:15)

The usual method of the author and/or editors of the Books of Kings would have been to follow the record of the reign of Ahaziah with materials concerning the reign of Jehoram, his brother. However, that method was deviated from to give special emphasis to the ministry of Elisha. Elisha, the successor of Elijah in prophetic ministry in Northern Israel, served first as Elijah's apprentice and then as prophet. Elisha began his ministry in the days of Ahab's reign (1 Kings 19:19-21) and continued at least until the beginning of Jehoash's reign (2 Kings 13:20). The reigns of the kings of Israel at least touched by Elisha totaled ninety-seven years (1 Kings 16:29; 22:51; 2 Kings 3:1; 10:36; 13:1,10). If we say that he followed Elijah in the nineteenth year of Ahab and died in the first year of Jehoash, Elisha still had an active ministry of over sixty-two or -three years.

Elijah's Translation and Elisha's Empowering (2:1-14)

Elijah, Elisha, and the sons of the prophets all knew that Elijah was about to depart from this life. Whether all or any of them understood that Elijah was to be translated to heaven without tasting death is not known. "From over you" (vv. 3,5) could imply that the sons of the prophets knew that Elijah would be caught up above Elisha into the heavens in some supernatural manner. However, most likely "from over you" means that Elijah would be removed as head prophet and that Elisha would serve in his place. Gilgal, Bethel, and Jericho were places where the sons of the prophets lived in special communities. Apparently, Elijah journeyed to these places on the day of his translation as a last act of encouragement of the sons of the prophets. Three times Elijah told Elisha to stay behind—at Gilgal, Bethel, and Jericho (vv. 2,4,6). The sons of the prophets also seemed to add their entreaties to Elijah's order in asking Elisha if he knew that the Lord that day would remove Elijah. Elisha's staying with Elijah reflects more than the loyal nature that qualified him to be Elijah's successor. It also reflects Elisha's determination to receive from Elijah the special power necessary for him to fulfill his role as Elijah's successor. Elisha's determination was rewarded in Elijah's asking Elisha what he wanted him to do for him before he was taken from him. Elijah's response indicated that Elisha's request for a double portion of his spirit was not his to give, but solely in the hands of God. He did, however, point to Elisha's seeing him translated as the sign by which he would know he had received his request.

Elijah was translated on the east side of the Jordan River after Elijah had used his mantle, that is, his hairy upper garment, miraculously to open the waters of the Jordan for him and Elisha to cross on dry ground (v. 8). The "whirlwind" (vv. 1,11) by which Elijah was caught up to heaven was a special wind in which God himself came to take Elijah to be with him. Elisha interpreted the "chariot of fire and horses of fire" (v. 11) that separated Elijah from him as symbolizing the national security that Elijah had provided. Israel suffered a great loss in Elijah's passing, for Elijah had been a defense more powerful than war chariots and their horses. All was not lost, however, for Elisha himself would become "the chariot of Israel and its horsemen" (2 Kings 13:14).

Elisha knew in seeing Elijah translated that he had received the double share of Elijah's spirit. His tearing of his clothes, a sign of grief, may also have symbolized his laying aside his garments to wear the garments of Elijah as his successor. Elijah demonstrated his faith in his God-given power by striking the waters of the Jordan with the mantle as Elijah had done and by commanding the waters to part in the name of the Lord God of Elijah. "Where is the Lord, the God of Elijah?" was an entreaty for God, who had clothed Elijah with power, to demonstrate that he also had clothed Elisha with power. The parting of the waters demonstrated that God indeed had empowered Elisha to serve as Elijah's successor.

Elisha's First Prophetic Appearance (2:15-18)

When the sons of the prophets saw the miracle Elisha wrought using the mantle of Elijah, they immediately recognized him to be the divinely appointed successor of Elijah (v. 15a). Their homage of him showed that they acknowledged him as their leader (v. 15b). After securing Elisha's reluctant consent to look for Elijah or his body, the sons of the prophets abandoned the fruitless search, after three days convinced that

God had miraculously transported him to heaven (vv. 16-17). The fruit-less search doubtless strengthened their faith in the leadership of Elisha who had told them not to go (v. 18).

Two Miracles of Elisha (2:19-25)

This section deals with two of the miraculous events that character-ized the life of Elisha. One was the healing of the waters of Jericho (vv. 19-22). The other was the awful punishment of the small, but contempt-ible boys of Bethel who blasphemed the prophet (vv. 23-25). Apparently, these events occurred shortly after the translation of Elijah and served to confirm Elisha as prophet in the eyes of the people of Israel.

Healing of the spring of Jericho (2:19-22).—"The men of the city" (v. 19) refer to the inhabitants of Jericho who would have learned from the sons of the prophets of Elisha's ability to work miracles. "Unfruitful" (v. 19) carries the idea of bereavement that stemmed from barrenness or abortion. Something in the water caused the trees either to be barren or to prematurely shed their fruit. The herds that fed on the herbage pro-duced by the water did not conceive or miscarried. The barrenness or abortion spread also to the people who drank the water. Some interpret the problem as being a carry-over of Joshua's curse upon those who re-built Jericho into a fortified city. The salt poured from the new dish into the water certainly did not in itself bring the permanent healing. God himself performed the miracle at the request of Elisha (v. 21). The new dish perhaps symbolized the purity and freshness of the healed waters. The salt with its ability to preserve and season symbolized the perma-nent sweetness of the healed waters. "Wholesome to this day" (v. 22) applied to the day of the author and/or editor. However, the spring, which today is called "Ain es-Sultan," continues to be a wonderful source of life to the plain of Jericho.

Cursing of the blaspheming boys (2:23-25).—Elisha journeyed from Jericho to Bethel, which was the chief seat of the idolatrous and licen-tious worship of the Lord God of Israel under the images of the golden calves. The "small boys" (v. 23), who came out of Bethel to jeer at Elisha, may have been younger teenagers according to the usage of the Hebrew word describing them. In blaspheming Elisha, they reflected the contemptible spirit of that community toward God and his true proph-ets. The twice repeated "Go up, you baldhead" (v. 23) probably carried some evil connotation. Elisha, who had approximately sixty years of ministry remaining, may have been prematurely bald. Possibly, he had some closely clipped or shaved spot (a tonsure) to designate his prophetic office. In any case, these boys knew Elisha the prophet and in insulting him blasphemed the prophets of God. "Cursed" (v. 24) carries the idea of judgment upon that which is trifling and contemptible by nature. In cursing them in the name of the Lord, he invoked on those trifling and contemptible boys the judgment of God to avenge the honor of his prophets. The Lord himself designated the punishment and caused the curse to be fulfilled in sending two she-bears out of the woods to injure forty-two of the boys. The purpose of the punishment was to cause the whole community to reverence the prophets of God, Elisha in particular.

Elisha and the Reign of Jehoram of Israel (3:1-27)

The reign of Jehoram the son of Ahab over Israel is now introduced. However, the ministry of Elisha continues to play the dominant role. After some introductory observations concerning the reign of Jehoram (3:1-3), this passage deals with Jehoram's military effort to reclaim Moab as a vassal of Israel and the establishment of Elisha on the national scene (3:4-27).

Introductory observations concerning Jehoram's reign (3:1-3).—Every king of northern Israel from its beginning with Jeroboam, the son of Nebat, was evil, and not one of them was ever commended as good. Jehoram is condemned less severely, because he was not as wicked as his father Ahab and his mother Jezebel (v. 2). The difference was in his rejection of Baal worship that had been introduced as the national religion by Ahab and zealously pressed upon the people of Israel by his mother, Jezebel. Apparently, he sought to purge the worship of Baal and to elevate once again as the national religion the worship of the Lord God of Israel under the idolatrous and licentious images of the golden calves introduced by Jeroboam the son of Nebat. "The pillar of Baal" (v. 2) that he removed was probably in the house of Baal in Samaria that had been erected and maintained by Ahab. He probably destroyed as well the image of Asherah (Baal's consort) that Ahab had also made and placed there. See comments on 1 Kings 16:32-33. His reforms, however, must not have been very successful, perhaps due to the continuing strong influence of Jezebel his mother. Certainly, Jehu found a thriving Baalism to destroy (2 Kings 10:10-28).

Jehoram's war to regain Moab; the establishment of Elisha as prophet on the national scene (3:4-27).—This passage provides an interesting insight into the tribute required of vassal nations. The annual tribute of Moab to Israel of one hundred thousand lambs and the wool of one hundred thousand lambs (v. 4) corresponds to Moab's being a land abounding in good pasture. Jehoram enlisted his vassal Jehoshaphat of Judah, who in turn enlisted his vassal Edom into a military coalition to regain for Israel rebellious Moab (vv. 5-7,9). The attack on Moab could have been made either by crossing the Jordan River north of the Dead Sea and striking south into Moab across the border river Arnon or by crossing south of the Dead Sea and entering the southern portion of Moab through the northern mountains of Edom. Jehoram chose to cross south of the Dead Sea, perhaps because the Moabites had strongly fortified cities in the northern section (v. 8). Their plan, however, had not counted on the drought that dried up the usual supplies of water in that area. Accordingly, after a circuitous march of seven days, Jehoram's army ran out of water (v. 9). Jehoram despaired, but Jehoshaphat encouraged the drought-plagued coalition to turn to Elisha for help (vv. 10-12). Elisha probably had been led by the Spirit of God to be in the vicinity, so that the three kings could turn to him.

The water that came without their seeing wind or rain probably resulted from a great rain in the eastern mountains of Edom (vv. 16-17). By the next morning, the water came from the direction of Edom until it had filled the dry streambeds where they were encamped (v. 20). The water that flowed through the red sandstone of "Edom," whose name means "red," looked like blood to the Moabite army who viewed it from the mountains high above (vv. 21-22). They surmised that the invading kings had turned on one another in brutal self-destruction of their army just as the coalition of the Moabites, Ammonites, and Edomites had destroyed one another in an invasion attempt of Judah (v. 23; 2 Chron. 20:22-23). Accordingly, the Moabite army left their secure place in the mountains and came into the valley to plunder the self-defeated army (v. 24). However, the Moabites themselves were slaughtered by the coalition army who pressed their victory until they had fulfilled Elisha's prophecy of overthrowing the Moabite cities, cutting down their fruit trees, stopping their springs of water, and ruining every good piece of land with stones (vv. 19-25).

The invasion ended with an unusual turn of events. The king of Moab, who faced certain defeat and death, sacrificed his firstborn son on the wall to Chemosh in full view for everyone to see, including the besieging army (vv. 26-27). "Great wrath upon Israel" (v. 27) probably is to be interpreted in terms of the effect of the sacrifice on the coalition army. Seemingly, when they beheld this plea to Chemosh for help, panic broke out among the coalition army in fear of Chemosh, and they fled back to their own land. Although Elisha's prophecy was fulfilled to the letter, the Israelites were not successful in regaining Moab as a vassal state.

Assorted Miracles and Other Experiences of Elisha (4:1 to 8:15).

The remainder of the material placed under the reign of Jehoram of Israel is devoted to assorted miracles and other experiences of Elisha. Apparently, all of these miracles and experiences took place during the reign of Jehoram. However, these miracles and experiences apparently are not listed necessarily in chronological order. If they were, then the experience of Gehazi before King Jehoram would be listed before Elisha's transfer forever to Gehazi and to his household the leprosy of Naaman (5:27; 8:1-6). The miracles particularly illustrate that Elisha was a kind and sympathetic man who used his ability to work miracles to meet human need and to honor the Lord God of Israel.

The increase of the widow's oil (4:1-7).—One of the sons of the prophets was involved in a transaction for which he had to borrow money. However, he died before he could pay off the debt, and his widow and two children were left in desperate straits. Specifically, the creditor was about to execute his right according to the law of Moses to force the children of the debtor to labor for him to pay off the debt (Lev. 25:39-40). The poor widow turned to Elisha for help, not only as the leader of the sons of the prophets, but especially as one who had both the power and the kindly disposition to help her (v. 1). The "jar of oil" (v. 2), which was the only item of value in the widow's house, was a flask of oil used for such tasks as anointing the body after washing. The miracle was performed by the power of God without the presence of Elisha (vv. 4-6). The miraculous oil, which stopped flowing only when there were no more vessels to fill, seemed limited only by the woman's faith in securing from the neighbors enough of the necessary empty vessels (v. 3). However, enough anointing oil was miraculously provided to pay off the debt when the oil was sold and to sustain the widow and her sons (v. 7). The miracle illustrates the care of God for those and their families who devote themselves wholeheartedly to the Lord. Note especially that the son of the prophet "feared the Lord" (v. 1).

A son for the Shunammite woman (4:8-37).—Elisha worked two miracles for the wealthy Shunammite woman who showed generosity toward him and his servant Gehazi. First, Elisha provided miraculous conception of a son for the Shunammite woman by her husband who was old (vv. 8-17). Second, Elisha healed the son who had died, presumably of a heat stroke (vv. 18-37). This double miracle illustrates the blessings that come to those who befriend a man of God.

Elisha lived in Mount Carmel where Elijah had called down the fire of God to consume the sacrifices (v. 25). However, in the execution of his ministry Elisha often passed through Shunem, which was located about sixteen miles south by southeast of Mount Carmel on the way to Jezreel. Elisha was assisted by his servant Gehazi, who perhaps performed for Elisha the same service Elisha had provided for Elijah. However, Gehazi proved not to have the character of a true man of God (2 Kings 5:20-27). Elisha's friendship with the wealthy Shunammite woman began in her providing food for Elisha and his servant whenever they passed that way (v. 8). When she detected that Elisha was indeed "a holy man of God" (v. 9), she and her husband built and furnished on the roof of their house a private room for Elisha's use (vv. 9-10). Elisha, touched by her kindness, asked her one day what favor he could do for her. She declined his offer to secure for her some special favor from the king or the commander of the army (v. 13a). Indeed, she declined any favor, saying that she lived securely among her own people without any need (v. 13b). Gehazi later suggested that Elisha utilize his prophetic powers to enable her to conceive by her husband who was old (v. 14). Although the Shunammite woman expressed polite skepticism at Elisha's prediction that she would bear a son about that time next year, she did later conceive of her husband and bore the promised son the following spring (vv. 16-17).

The story moves ahead several years to the time when the young son was smitten in the field where he had gone with his father to participate in the harvest (v. 18). The first symptoms of his sunstroke were severe pains in the head (v. 19a). When the son died shortly thereafter in his mother's arms, she immediately went to Mount Carmel to solicit Elisha's help (vv. 19b-25). "It is neither new moon nor sabbath" (v. 23) suggests that these were the main days of worship for the people. With the words "It will be well" (v. 23), the woman expressed her faith that Elisha would bring healing to their son. Note that "well" means "wholeness or peace."

Elisha first attempted but failed to heal the son by sending his servant ahead to place his prophetic staff on the face of the child (v. 29). Some suggest that this attempt failed because of the mother's lack of faith in refusing to go back without Elijah (v. 30). In stretching himself out on the child (v. 34), Elisha may have followed the method of Elijah in healing the son of the widow of Zarephath (1 Kings 17:21). Whatever the method, the healing was wrought by the power of God through Elisha's prayer (v. 33). Elisha's stretching himself upon the child so that his mouth was upon his mouth and so forth probably symbolized that the God-given power in Elisha's life was being transferred miraculously to the child (vv. 34-35). The elapsed time between the death of the child and Elisha's arrival negates the possibility of restoration by artificial respiration. The woman in gratitude worshiped God who had wrought the miracle through his servant Elisha (v. 37).

Curing the death in the pot (4:38-41).—Elisha miraculously made the poisonous pottage wholesome on one of his routine trips to the sons of the prophets who lived in Gilgal. "A famine in the land" (v. 38a) perhaps refers to the seven-year famine Elisha predicted (2 Kings 8:1). "Sitting before him" (v. 38b) means that the sons of the prophets were assembled before Elisha for instructions. In preparation for their need of food, Elisha commanded "his servant" (v. 38c), who may have been Gehazi but more likely one of the sons of the prophets, to prepare a great pot of pottage for their meal. Another servant went into the field to gather edible herbs for the pottage and brought back a lap full of "wild gourds" (v. 39) from a vine growing in the open field. "Gourds" basically describes that which when pressed cracks open with a loud noise, exposing its seeds. "Wild gourds" has been interpreted as wild cucumbers with strong purgative qualities. Perhaps the bitter taste, which is often a natural characteristic of inedible food, signaled the danger in the pot. Elisha probably threw meal in the pot not as an antidote to the poisonous cucumbers, but to symbolize the wholesome change wrought in the pot by the power of God at his request.

Feeding a hundred men (4:42-44).—The setting for this miracle was most likely still at Gilgal during the famine or at some other community of the sons of the prophets. Twenty loaves of barley bread and some fresh ears of corn were brought to Elisha by a man as the firstfruits of his crop. This is an example of how the "seven thousand" who had not bowed the knee to Baal or to the golden calves continued to adhere to the command of Moses to give the firstfruits of their land to the servants of God to sustain them (Num. 18:13; Deut. 18:1-5). Elisha, in turn, commanded that the bread and the corn should be used to feed the one hundred men with him. The insufficiency of the provision to feed one hundred men is indicated first in that the man himself brought the bread and the corn in a sack and second in the exclamation of the servant that he could never feed one hundred men with that small amount. Elisha, however, repeated the command to use it to feed the one hundred men and predicted that all would eat of it to their fill and have some left over. This miracle is similar to Christ's feeding the multitude with the five loaves and the two fishes with this notable exception: Elisha predicted the miracle that was wrought by the power of God, whereas Christ himself multiplied the loaves and the fishes (John 6:8-14).

Healing of Naaman (5:1-19).—Verse 1 provides a fourfold description of Naaman's greatness. He was the number one military leader of the nation of Syria. He was held in highest esteem by his master, Ben-hadad king of Syria. He was highly honored by the people of Syria for the great military victory the Lord, who providentially controls in his universal power the rise and fall of all nations, had given to Syria through Naaman's leadership. He was personally a mighty warrior of great ability and courage. But all of his greatness was marred by his being a leper.

The root idea of leprosy, which is "to strike down," denotes the tragic nature of the disease. Basically, leprosy was an eruptive skin disease that contaminated the bloodstream, producing a thickening and deterioration of the tissues and nerves. In its worst form, leprosy mutilated the body and often resulted in death. Naaman apparently was in the earliest stages of this dread disease. However, if he had the worst kind of leprosy, he could look forward to his hair falling out, to his fingers and toes falling off, to his gums being absorbed and his teeth falling out, to mutilation of his eyes, nose, and palate, and to other disfigurements of his body. The fact that Naaman was not already barred from society suggests a different attitude toward lepers among the Syrians than among the Israelites who immediately quarantined or expelled the leper from society. Although we have medicine today to cure leprosy, there was no known cure in the ancient Near East.

Naaman, however, was given hope by the testimony of an Israelite slave girl in his household that there was a prophet in Samaria who could and would heal him (vv. 2-3). Naaman then came to King Jehoram in Samaria, armed with a letter from King Ben-hadad of Syria demanding that King Jehoram heal Naaman (vv. 4-6). The presents Naaman brought as a reward for his healing were worth a small fortune, figured by modern values of gold and silver (v. 5b). When Elisha heard of King Jehoram's despair at the demand of the king of Syria, Elisha agreed to heal Naaman in order that Naaman would come to know by his personal experience that Elisha was a true prophet of the one true God (v. 8).

Naaman almost missed being healed because of his initial unwillingness to follow Elisha's simple command to dip himself seven times in the Jordan River for healing (vv. 9-12). Naaman was angry for three reasons. First, he resented Elisha—whom he held to be his inferior—not coming out to him. Second, he resented Elisha not performing some spectacular healing ritual over him. Third, he resented the demand that he wash in the unattractive Jordan River. But when he humbly complied with Elisha's command, he was completely healed (vv. 13-14).

Naaman, soundly converted, showed his gratitude for healing in his returning to Elisha to confess his personal faith in the Lord God of Israel as the one and only true God and to present Elisha with the gifts (v. 15). Elisha refused the gifts apparently to show that the gracious healing of God could not be bought (v. 16). The request of Naaman for some of the soil of Israel to take back to Syria with him probably implies that Naaman, who had come to recognize the Lord God of Israel alone to be God, still had the limited view that God could only be worshiped properly at an altar built with dirt from Israel (v. 17a). Naaman, who vowed to worship only the Lord (v. 17b), also requested God's forgiveness for his having to accompany in the line of duty his master into the house of Rimmon (v. 18). Rimmon, another name for Hadad the chief god of Syria, was thought to be supremely a storm god. Elisha's "Go in peace" apparently means that the prophet granted both of Naaman's requests.

Leprosy transferred to Gehazi (5:20-27).—The miraculous transfer of Naaman's leprosy to Gehazi and to his descendants forever (v. 27) provides a stern warning to men of God lest they exploit their prophetic office for material gain. Gehazi's sin illustrates that "the love of money is the root of all evils" (1 Tim. 6:10). Elisha's miraculous powers are also seen in his going in spirit with Gehazi to detect crime and in his reading Gehazi's mind as to what he intended to do with the ill-gotten gain (v. 26). "Was it a time" (v. 26) suggests that under other circumstances Elisha might have received gifts from Naaman. But Naaman needed to be taught that God's gracious healing could not be bought, and he had been so impressed by the lesson that he had given his total self to the Lord God of Israel. Gehazi's avarice in the name of Elisha placed Elisha in the category of the religious charlatans who use their spiritual gifts for selfish gain.

Floating ax head (6:1-7).—This passage shows how the sons of the prophets dwelt together in their prophetic community. "Under your charge" (v. 1) means that Elisha was the leader of the sons of the prophets and not necessarily that he dwelt there with them. Prophetic communities were located at Gilgal (about seven miles north by northwest of Bethel), at Bethel, and at Jericho. Going to the Jordan to secure the timber needed for expansion suggests that this prophetic dwelling was in Jericho (v. 2). The need to expand their dwelling place illustrates the growth of the sons of the prophets under Elisha's leadership. The loss of the ax head was more grievous in that it was borrowed (v. 5). Elisha used the stick, which would float on the water, to symbolize what he wanted the ax head to do (v. 6). Accordingly, through the power of God, it floated to the top where the servant retrieved it (v. 7).

Capture of the Syrian army (6:8-23).—The capture of the Syrian army involved four miracles. First was Elisha's miraculous ability to know the plans of the Syrians in sending various raiding parties into Israel (vv. 8-12). The testimony of the servants of the king of Syria to him of Elisha's ability to know even his most secret thoughts and conversations (vv. 11-12) was of particular significance. Second was the miraculous revelation to the servant of Elisha (apparently someone other than Gehazi) of the great host of heaven that surrounded and protected Elisha from the Syrian horses and chariots and foot soldiers who had come to take Elisha to King Ben-hadad (vv. 13-17). The superior heavenly "horses and chariots of fire" (v. 17) protecting Elisha were already present before his prayer. The prayer was for his servant, who feared for Elisha's and his life, to have his eyes opened to recognize that God had provided a heavenly host for their protection superior to the Syrian host. This illustrates that God as the Lord of hosts provides superior heavenly forces for all who are obedient to him. The third miracle was the blindness with which the Syrian army was smitten at the prayer of Elisha to the Lord (vv. 18-19). The fourth miracle was the restoration of the sight of the Syrian army once Elisha had them in Samaria surrounded by the army of Israel (vv. 19-20). Jehoram humbly asking Elisha concerning the fate of the prisoners and his calling Elisha "my father" (v. 21) indicate the great reverence in which Elisha was held even by this ungodly king of Israel. Elisha forbade putting to death the army he miraculously captured, inasmuch as they should receive the same merciful treatment normally given prisoners of war (v. 22). After providing a lavish meal for the captives, Elisha released them to return to Ben-hadad with their testimony of Elisha's miraculous power and of his graciousness (v. 23). In thwarting the plans of the Syrian raiding parties and in capturing their army, Elisha illustrated that he was indeed "the chariots of Israel, and its horsemen" (2 Kings 13:14). The effect of Elisha's intervention was that the king of Syria sent no more raiding parties into Israel (v. 23c). Ben-hadad did, however, later mount an all-out attack on Israel, as is indicated in the record of the siege of Samaria by Ben-hadad.

Deliverance of besieged Samaria (6:24 to 7:20).—There were several Ben-hadads who served as kings of Syria (8:7-15; 13:3). The Ben-hadad who here besieged Samaria was probably the Ben-hadad who previously besieged Samaria, who was defeated by and submitted himself to Ahab, who later commanded the army that killed Ahab, and who finally was assassinated by Hazael who reigned in his stead (1 Kings 20:20; 2 Kings 8:15). The king of Israel at the time of this siege was most likely Jehoram, the son of Ahab, as the present position of the record suggests.

The siege in time produced a great famine in the city of Samaria (6:24-31). The famine was so severe that the people paid exorbitant prices for forbidden and undesirable food like an ass's head and even for the refuse of the pigeon (v. 25). (The Jews reportedly ate the dung of animals during the siege of Jerusalem by the Romans under Titus.) Most horrible was the eating of children even by their mothers (vv. 26-29). King Jehoram, who had clothed himself humbly in sackcloth hoping to get God to relieve the siege, may have vowed to kill Elisha because Elisha had encouraged the king to hold out against the Syrians with a promise of help from the Lord (vv. 30-31,33).

Elisha miraculously saw and understood the purpose of the messenger sent by Jehoram to kill him (v. 32). In referring to Jehoram as "this murderer" (v. 32), literally, "this son of a murderer," Elisha probably had in mind Jehoram being the son of Ahab, who had killed Naboth. Jehoram showed himself also to be a murderer in designing to kill Elisha. "Why should I wait for the Lord any longer?" (v. 33) indicates that Jehoram had given up on the Lord's helping them and was about to surrender to the Syrians. Elisha, however, predicted immediate relief from the famine, so that by the next day good food could be purchased at the gate of Samaria for reasonable prices (7:1). The prediction of the unbelieving captain's death after he had seen, but before he had participated in the relief of the famine, may not involve punishment for his doubting the prophecy (7:2). Perhaps Elisha simply announced what he was able to see concerning the future of the captain.

The four lepers who sought to save their lives by surrendering to the Syrians discovered the hastily abandoned camp of the besieging Syrians (7:3-8). The miraculous rout of the Syrians seemingly was first brought on by the Lord's causing them to believe the rumor that the Israelites had hired the armies of the kings of the Hittites and of the kings of Egypt to break the siege. Then the Lord caused them to imagine that they heard the approach of a great army composed of war chariots, horsemen, and foot soldiers (7:6). The result was that they fled in absolute panic, leaving behind all of their supplies (7:7). The four lepers ate to their fill and gathered valuables from the abandoned tents until they began to fear that punishment would come upon them if they delayed even until morning sharing the spoils of the Syrians with those shut up in the city (7:8-9). Although Jehoram feared that the abandoned camp was a trick to draw them out of the city, the scouts confirmed that the Syrian army had indeed miraculously fled in absolute rout beyond the Jordan River (7:10-15). The people surged out of the city to plunder the camp, and Elisha's prophecy came to pass concerning a measure of fine flour for a shekel and two measures of barley for a shekel (7:16). His prediction concerning the unbelieving captain also came to pass (7:17-20). The captain saw with his own eyes the relief of the famine, but he was trampled to death at the gate of Samaria by the starving people before he got a chance to eat of the food.

Restoration of the land of the Shunammite woman (8:1-6).—This passage records the continued blessings that came to the Shunammite woman because of her kindness to Elisha. Elisha saw and probably predicted the seven-year famine that the Lord had caused to come upon the land of Israel. At Elisha's advice to leave her home to dwell in some foreign land for the time of the famine, the woman dwelt with her household for seven years in the land of the Philistines. Either before or during her sojourn in the land of the Philistines, her husband died. The widow returned to her home and discovered that either the crown, her nearest of kin, or someone else had taken possession of her property. Miraculously, the widow appeared to the king with a request for restoration of the property to her at exactly the same time Gehazi, the servant of Elisha, was relating to King Jehoram how Elisha had restored the widow's son to life. As a favor to Elisha, the king granted her legal right to repossess her property and even decreed that she should receive all that the property produced while she was away. Even if the property had been sold for some debt upon it, the property was to revert to the widow and her son at the end of the seventh year (Ex. 21:2; Deut. 15:1-2). The court official whom the king sent with her was to see that the king's decree was carried out. Although Gehazi's leprosy may have been of such a nature that he could continue to associate with people (2 Kings 5:1-5), most likely this experience took place before the transfer of Naaman's leprosy to Gehazi and to his household (2 Kings 5:27).

Elisha and the Syrian coup (8:7-15).—Elisha perhaps had gone to Damascus to carry out God's command to Elijah to anoint Hazael to be king of Syria (1 Kings 19:15). As noted before, Hazael would be God's instrument in punishing Israel for their sin of calf worship and of Baalism. When Ben-hadad, king of Syria, who was sick, heard of Elisha being in Damascus, he sent Hazael, one of his trusted servants, to inquire of the prophet as to whether he would recover from his sickness (vv. 7-8). Elisha's words, "You shall certainly recover," (v. 10) should be interpreted to mean that the illness itself was not fatal and that, given sufficient time, he would recover from the illness. Elisha, however, perceived that Ben-hadad would certainly die. Doubtless, Elisha had in mind that Ben-hadad had been devoted to the Lord for destruction. Although he had escaped God's judgment in wicked Ahab's violation of God's most holy decree, Ben-hadad would die.

While talking with Hazael, Elisha went into a prophetic trance in which he saw Hazael as king of Syria desolating the people of Israel (vv. 11-13). Hazael's humble conception of himself as "but a dog" has its parallel in Assyrian inscriptions when he is referred to as "son of a nobody." He was, however, the one God had chosen to execute wrath upon Israel for their sins and also the one God had chosen to execute judgment on Ben-hadad. On the day after he returned to deliver Elisha's message to Ben-hadad, Hazael assassinated the king and seized the throne for himself. Moreover, when he became king, he desolated Israel, as perceived by Elisha (2 Kings 10:32; 13:3,22-23).

The Reign of Jehoram of Judah (8:16-24)

Jehoram the son of Jehoshaphat who reigned in his stead should not be confused with Jehoram (Joram) the son of Ahab whose reign we have just considered. "Joram" (vv. 16,21,25) is an alternate spelling of Jehoram. The reign of Jehoram illustrates the tragedy of the marriage alliance between good king Jehoshaphat and wicked king Ahab by which Jehoshaphat, for the sake of peace with Israel, secured Athaliah the daughter of Ahab and Jezebel to be the wife of his son Jehoram. Under the wicked influence of Athaliah, Jehoram walked in the evil "ways of the kings of Israel, as the house of Ahab had done" (v. 18), murdered his brothers and some of the princes of Judah (2 Chron. 21:4), led the people of Judah and Jerusalem into unfaithfulness (2 Chron. 21:13), brought a great plague upon his people, his children, his wives, and all his possessions (2 Chron. 21:14), and death by a severe intestinal disease upon himself (2 Chron. 21:15). Part of the plague was the invasion of Judah by the Philistines and the Arabs that resulted in the loss of Jehoram's possessions, of his sons and of his wives, so that only Jehoahaz his youngest son (called Ahaziah) was left (2 Chron. 21:16-17). The nation of Judah itself was saved from destruction only because of God's faithfulness to his covenant with David to give him a son forever upon the throne of David in Jerusalem (v. 19; 1 Kings 11:36). The revolt of Edom and Libnah, which weakened the kingdom of Judah, were additional results of God's judgment upon wicked Jehoram (vv. 20-22).

The Beginning of the Reign of Ahaziah of Judah (8:25-29)

The evil reign and violent death of Ahaziah the grandson of Jehoshaphat after one year on the throne is another illustration of the tragic results of the unholy marriage alliance of Jehoshaphat with Ahab by which Athaliah the daughter of Ahab and Jezebel came into the royal family of David. Ahaziah, who is elsewhere called Jehoahaz (2 Chron. 21:17), was the youngest and only living son of Jehoram and Athaliah after the massacre of their family. Ahaziah was twenty-two years of age when he began to reign (v. 26). The reference in 2 Chronicles 22:2 to his being forty-two at the time of his ascension to the throne is due to a copyist's error. His mother Athaliah is here spoken of as "a granddaughter of Omri" (v. 26) to show that her wicked roots went back to Omri, the founder of their evil house. She counseled Ahaziah in wickedness, just as she had Jehoram her husband (2 Chron. 22:3). Ahaziah also continued the wicked military alliances with the house of Ahab that had been begun by Jehoshaphat his grandfather and fostered by Jehoram his father. Reference here to Ahaziah's coalition with Jehoram of Israel against Hazael of Syria at Ramoth-gilead shows how Ahaziah happened to be in Jezreel where he met violent death at the hands of Jehu, the avenger of God (vv. 28-29; 9:27-28). The death of Ahaziah, the sons of his brothers, and their guardians was God's judgment upon Ahaziah and upon his father Jehoram for their wicked alliance with the house of Ahab (2 Chron. 22:7-9). Just as they followed the house of Ahab in their wicked ways, so they died with them under the judgment of God. Their execution was within the commission of Jehu, since they were grandsons and great-grandsons of Ahab (2 Kings 9:4-10).

The Revolt and Reign of Jehu: The End of the House of Omri and the Purge of Baalism (9:1 to 10:36)

The Anointing and Commissioning of Jehu (9:1-10)

While the combined armies of Israel and Judah were encamped against the Syrians before Ramoth-gilead, Elisha fulfilled the last of the commissions that Elijah had received from the Lord at Mount Horeb (1 Kings 19:16). He sent one of his disciples to Ramoth-gilead to anoint Jehu to be king of Israel and to commission him to destroy the house of

Ahab. Implicit in the command to destroy the house of Ahab was the purging from the nation the worship of Baal that Ahab and Jezebel had pressed upon the people as the state religion.

Jehu was the son of Jehoshaphat (not the king) and the grandson of Nimshi, but he was often called the son of Nimshi (1 Kings 19:16; 2 Kings 9:2,14,20). He had been a trusted soldier in the service of Ahab (2 Kings 9:25), and the reference of the prophet to him as "O commander" (v. 5) seems to single him out as the commander of the combined armies. For the significance of the anointing ceremony, see comments on 1 Kings 1:34. The private anointing of Jehu follows the pattern of Samuel's secret anointing of Saul (1 Sam. 10:1); however, Samuel anointed David in the presence of his brothers (1 Sam. 16:13), and Nathan publicly anointed Solomon (1 Kings 1:34). In anointing Jehu as "king over the people of the Lord" (v. 6), the prophet indicated that God still considered Israel to be his people. Although they had forsaken him, he had not forsaken them. Indeed, the Kings material recounts greater prophetic activity among the faithless people of Israel than among the more faithful people of Judah. For an interpretation of the predicted destruction of the house of Ahab, see comments on 1 Kings 21:19-24. Carrying out the command of Elisha to "open the door and flee" (vv. 3,10) added mystery to the anointing and commissioning and prevented the prophet from being involved in discussion or other affairs.

Proclamation of Jehu as King (9:11-13)

When the fellow commanders understood that Jehu had been anointed and commissioned by God to be king, they improvised a throne on the bare steps, blew the coronation trumpet, and joined in the customary cry "Jehu is king" (v. 13). The derisive reference to the prophet as "this mad fellow" (v. 11) was perhaps occasioned by the aburpt, even weird way in which the prophet delivered his message to Jehu. However, in Jehu's saying, "You know the fellow and his talk" (v. 11), he may have implied that this prophet was known to all of them as one characterized by unusual ecstatic utterance. The respect that they had, however, for his message is indicated in their rising up to follow Jehu in his revolt against the house of Ahab.

Assassinations That Ended the House of Omri and Purged Israel of Baalism (9:14 to 10:27)

Of Jehoram (9:14-26).—Jehu immediately went to work as God's avenger against the house of Omri/Ahab. His first step was to go to Jezreel to put Jehoram to death. There Jehoram was recuperating from wounds received in his battle with Hazael of Syria for the possession of Ramoth-gilead (vv. 14-16). Whether he knew at the time that Ahaziah of Judah was there visiting with Jehoram is not known (v. 16). With the words, "If this is your mind" (v. 15a), Jehu said in effect to his commanders, "If you stand with me in conspiracy to destroy the house of Omri and to make me king." "Then let no one slip out of the city to go and tell the news in Jezreel" (v. 15b) implies that Ramoth-gilead was at that time in the possession of the Israelites and that Jehu wanted steps to be taken to ensure the secrecy of their plot against Jehoram.

The furious driving of Jehu is proverbial. "Furiously" (v. 20) is the same root as "mad fellow" (v. 11), and "drives furiously" carries the idea of driving like a mad man. Jehu, however, may not have been driving his chariot as fast as imagined, since there was time enough between Jehu's being spotted by the watchman and his arrival at the city itself for the two riders and then for Jehoram and Ahaziah to go out to the approaching party (vv. 17-21). Jehoram and Ahaziah themselves probably went out because they feared Jehu was bringing bad news from the battle front.

Jehu's response to Jehoram's, "Is it peace" (v. 22), left no doubt as to the intentions of Jehu and his soldiers. The "harlotries" (v. 22) of Jezebel, which refer to the idolatrous practices of Baalism, certainly implied the licentious acts involved in the "sacred" prostitution of Baalism. The major thought, however, was that Jezebel in leading Israel into the apostasy of Baalism had led the people away from the Lord, Israel's true husband. The "sorceries" (v. 22) of Jezebel refer to the incantations and charms by which the favors of Baal were sought and the people were seduced into Baal worship. The body of Jehoram was thrown on the property of Naboth to show that Jehoram's life had been taken to avenge the murder of Naboth (v. 26). In accord with the prophecy of Elijah, the body of Jehoram probably remained exposed until it was eaten by the vultures (1 Kings 21:24).

Of Ahaziah (9:27-29).—Jehu put Ahaziah to death because he was the grandson of Ahab and Jezebel. However, his body was spared mutilation and given a royal burial in Jerusalem because of the godly influence of his grandfather Jehoshaphat (2 Chron. 22:9). For additional comments as to why Ahaziah was killed, see 2 Kings 8:25-29. Whether Ahaziah began reigning in the eleventh (9:29) or the twelfth year (8:25) of Jehoram's reign depends on the method of figuring the beginning of Jehoram's reign.

Of Jezebel (9:30-37).—Although very little time had elapsed between the death of Jehoram and Jehu's arrival at the gate of Jezreel, Jezebel had already heard of Jehu's conspiracy (v. 30). She prepared herself in her best royal regalia and defiantly confronted Jehu (vv. 30-31). Perhaps she was so careful about her adornment because of her belief that her bodily appearance in the next world would be a continuation of the way she looked at death. "Is it peace?" (v. 31) was nothing more than a sarcastic greeting. She identified Jehu with Zimri, who reigned only seven days after he assassinated the king before he was overthrown by Omri and took his own life, probably to warn Jehu of the fate he would bring upon himself by executing the king (1 Kings 16:10-19). The roles of Zimri and Jehu were alike in that both operated under the providence of God to bring an evil house to its destruction.

At Jehu's command, several men threw Jezebel out of the window through which she had been looking down at him. The fall certainly mutilated Jezebel and probably killed her (v. 33). Jehu drove his horses and chariot over her battered body so that it could be said that "they trampled her" (v. 33). "Cursed woman" (v. 34) meant that Jezebel had been marked by God for destruction because of her sin. After Jehu had taken over the palace and had been treated to a meal, he remembered the need to bury Jezebel since she was the daughter of Ethbaal, king of Sidon (v. 34). However, by this time, the dogs of Jezreel had devoured her body, in fulfillment of the prophecy of Elijah (vv. 35-37; 1 Kings 21:23).

Of Ahab's sons and supporters (10:1-11).—"Sons" is used in the wider sense to include grandsons and so forth. "Seventy sons" is most likely a round number standing for all the male descendants of Ahab. Jehu instigated their death by two letters. In the first (vv. 1-3), he challenged the guardians of Ahab's sons and the rulers of the city of Samaria to choose the ablest of Ahab's sons for their king and to fight it out with him to determine who would be king of Israel. In fear of Jehu's power, they refused the challenge and committed themselves to follow Jehu with the promise to do whatever he commanded (vv. 4-5). Jehu commanded them in the second letter to assassinate the sons of Ahab and to present themselves to him at Jezreel along with the heads of Ahab's sons (v. 6). When they came with the heads, Jehu commanded that the heads be placed at the entrance of the gate to Jezreel where they could be found the next morning (vv. 7-8).

The city gate was the place of judgment, and the presence there of the severed heads could imply that the people of Jezreel were guilty of their murder. Jehu first declared their innocency of the deed and then acknowledged that he had killed Jehoram (v. 9). With the question "But who struck down all these?" (v. 9) Jehu implied that the death of Ahab's sons (as well as his killing Ahaziah) had come about as the result of the providence of God to fulfill Elijah's prediction that all the house of Ahab should be utterly swept away. "Know then that there shall fall to the earth nothing of the word of the Lord" (v. 10) is Jehu's acknowledgment of what God had already done to fulfill Elijah's prophecy and his pledge to continue the purge until every member of the house of Ahab had been killed. The summary statement "so Jehu slew" (v. 11) anticipates the death of those yet remaining of Ahab's house. "All his great men, and his familiar friends, and his priests" (v. 11) refers to supporters of the house of Ahab.

Of kinsmen of Ahaziah (10:12-14).—Ahaziah, the king of Judah whom Jehu slew (9:27-28), was Ahab's grandson. "The kinsmen of Ahaziah," such as certain nephews and cousins, were also relatives of Ahab and, thus, under the judgment of God. The providence of God in searching out for destruction every member of Ahab's house is seen in Jehu's meeting these in the way as he went from Jezreel to Samaria.

Of Ahab's descendants in Samaria (10:15-17).—On his way to Samaria to execute the remaining members of the house of Ahab, Jehu met Jehonadab. Jehonadab was himself a devoted follower of the Lord God of Israel and one in heart with Jehu in his determination to purge the land of the house of Ahab and the religion of Baal (v. 15b). Jehu perhaps asked Jehonadab to ride in his chariot with him to demonstrate that his purge was not motivated by mere selfish ambition, but by an earnest desire to return to the true worship of the Lord (vv. 15c-16). However, see 2 Kings 10:28-31 to note that Jehu did not truly worship the Lord.

Jehonadab was the founder of the Rechabites, whom he named in honor of his father Rechab. Rechab, like the father-in-law of Moses, was a Kenite (Judg. 1:16; 1 Chron. 2:55). Jehonadab encouraged his sons, daughters, and so forth not to drink wine, build houses, sow seed, or plant a vineyard, but to dwell in tents throughout their days (Jer. 35:5-10). Their purpose was (1) to preserve the simplicity and purity of Israel's ancient life and (2) to protest Israel's identity with the ways of Canaan. Because of their loyalty to their father's wishes, God promised them that they would always have descendants who would stand before him in loyalty and honor (Jer. 35:18-19).

Jehu continued on his way to Samaria where he put to death the remaining members of the house of Ahab. The prophecy of Elijah concerning the absolute destruction of the house of Ahab was thus complete

(v. 17). There remained only to purge from the nation the devotees of Baal whose worship had been encouraged, indeed pressed on Israel by Jezebel.

Of devotees of Baal (10:18-27).—Under the guise of serving Baal and honoring his devotees more than Ahab, Jehu assembled in Samaria and put to death all the worshipers of Baal (vv. 18-25). In the King James Version the distinction made between the "images of Baal" (v. 26) that Jehu burned and the pillar that he destroyed is made clearly. The "images" (KJV, v. 26) that Jehu burned were probably lesser representatives of Baal and his consort. The pillar that he demolished was probably of stone and the chief statue of Baal. "Latrine," which is literally "a place of dung" (Deut. 23: 12-14), carries the larger idea of a cesspool. The action degraded Baal and forever contaminated the site as a place of worship.

Appraisal of Jehu's Reign (10:28-31)

Jehu was praised for his obedience to God in wiping Baalism from Israel (v. 28). However, Hosea the prophet pronounced judgment upon the house of Jehu "for the blood of Jezreel" (Hos. 1:4), which doubtless had to do with Jehu's ruthless methods and his impure motives in exterminating the house of Ahab. Also, Jehu failed to follow through in obedience with all of his heart to the law of the Lord God of Israel as given by Moses (v. 31). His sin was in failing to turn from the golden calf worship of Jeroboam the son of Nebat by which idolatry and licentiousness were introduced into the worship of the Lord. See comments on 1 Kings 12:25-33. God rewarded Jehu for his obedience in purging Israel of the house of Ahab and of Baalism by promising to cause his sons to reign on the throne of Israel for four generations (v. 30). God's promise was fulilled in the reigns of Jehoahaz, Jehoash (Joash), Jeroboam II, and Zechariah (2 Kings 15:12). Altogether Jehu and his sons reigned over Israel a total of more than one hundred and two years (2 Kings 10:36; 13:1; 13:10; 14:23; 15:8).

The Lord's Beginning to Cut Off Parts of Israel (10:32-33)

In Jehu's day, the Lord began to take away the Promised Land from his people because of their sin (v. 32). The instrument of the Lord's chastisement was Hazael, king of Syria, who had been anointed by God to punish Israel for her sin. See comment on 1 Kings 19:11-17. In accord with Elisha's prophecy (2 Kings 8:12-13), Hazael devastated the land of Israel (v. 32b). He took from them all of the Promised Land east of the

Jordan (v. 33). This area had been alloted to Reuben, Gad, and the half-tribe of Manasseh. How tragic that Jehu did not turn to the Lord with all his heart so that he could give him and his sons not only longevity of rule, but fullness of blessings in the Promised Land.

Concluding Observations Concerning Jehu's Reign (10:34-36)

Archaeology gives us an insight into "the acts of Jehu" (v. 34) not found in the Kings or Chronicles material. The Black Obelisk of Shalmanezer III pictures Jehu kneeling before the Assyrian king. The cuneiform text tells of the silver and gold and costly vessels that Jehu brought in tribute. Doubtless, Jehu sought the help of the Assyrian against the Syrians. How much better it would have been for him to have sought the help of God by wholehearted obedience to his law.

The Reign of Jehoash of Judah (11:1 to 12:21)

The Usurpation of Athaliah the Mother of Ahaziah (11:1-3)

Athaliah was the daughter of Ahab and Jezebel, who became the wife of Jehoram, the son of Jehoshaphat, the king of Judah, as the result of the unholy marriage alliance fostered by Jehoshaphat with Ahab of Israel. This passage, which shows how Athaliah all but annihilated the royal seed of David, is another illustration of the tragic results of that unholy alliance. See comments on 2 Kings 8:25-29. When Athaliah saw that Jehu had killed her son, she seized the throne as queen mother and killed all of the royal family except Jehoash (Joash) the baby son of Ahaziah, who was hidden by Jehosheba in the house of the Lord for the six years of Athaliah's reign (vv. 1-3). "All the royal family" (v. 1) refers, of course, to those who remained after the slaughter by Jehu of "the kinsmen of Ahaziah" (10:13-14). Jehosheba was most likely not the daughter of Jehoram by Athaliah, but only Ahaziah's half-sister (v. 2; 2 Chron. 22:11). She was also the wife of Jehoiada, the high priest (2 Chron 22:11).

The Coronation of Jehoash and the Execution of Athaliah (11:4-16)

Jehoïada, the high priest who was the uncle of Jehoash by his marriage to Jehosheba, plotted the coronation of Jehoash (vv. 4-12) and the execution of Athaliah (vv. 13-16). "The Carites" (v. 4) were members of the royal bodyguard who got their name from their ancient homeland of Crete. Note comments on 1 Kings 1:33. "Crown" (v. 12), like the word *Nazirite*, has the basic idea of consecration. Accordingly, the crown symbolized ideally the king's consecration of himself to God and to his task of ruling over the people in the Spirit of God according to God's law. "Testimony" (v. 12) refers to the copy of the law that the king was to make for himself from the Book of the Law (Deut. 17:18-20). He was to keep it before him and to read it all the days of his life. It was called "the testimony," because it bore constant witness to his covenant obligations to fear God and to know and do all the words of the law. It also reminded the king of the blessings that would come upon him and the people for obedience to the law of God, but the curses that would result from their disobedience.

The Renewal of the Covenant and Enthronement of the King (11:17-20)

While still in the house of God, and immediately following the coronation of the king and the execution of Athaliah, Jehoiada cut a twofold covenant (v. 17). The first was a renewal of the covenant between the Lord, the king, and the people by which the king and the people committed themselves to "be the Lord's people," that is, to live according to the law of God which was in the hand of the king as the testimony. The second was between the king and the people by which the king committed himself to rule the people according to the law of God and by which the people pledged themselves to obey the king as the God-appointed ruler. To implement this covenant, Jehoiada led them to take three additional steps. The first was to destroy the house of Baal, his altars and images, and to execute the priests of Baal (v. 18; Deut. 17:2-7). The second was to set "watchmen" (v. 18b), that is, priests and Levites, in the house of God to ensure that the worship of God was in accord with the law of Moses. Finally, they led the coronation procession to the king's house where Jehoash, the child king, took his seat upon the throne as God's representative (vv. 19-20).

Observations Concerning Jehoash's Reign (11:21 to 12:21)

"Nevertheless" (12:3) points to the limitations in Jehoash's ministry as a godly king. First, he failed to lead the people to forsake their local sanctuaries that stood in violation to God's command to sacrifice only in the Temple at Jerusalem. Second, he allowed himself at Jehoiada's death to be influenced by the princes of Judah to return to the worship of Baal that was introduced in Judah by the wicked queen Athaliah (2 Chron. 24:17-18). Third, he refused to heed the call of the prophets to repentance (2 Chron. 24:19). Fourth, Jehoash put to death the prophet Zechariah, who was the son of Jehoiada, for speaking against his sins (2

Chron. 24:20-22). His murder of Zechariah resulted in his being assassinated at the age of forty-eight, after a reign of forty-one years (2 Chron. 24:25).

Jehoash's good work was to repair the house of God, which had been broken into and ransacked for the worship of Baal by those who followed the wicked queen Athaliah (2 Chron. 24:7). His plan was for the priests to utilize for the repair "all the money of the holy things . . . brought into the house of the Lord" (12:4), which included the assessed poll tax (Ex. 30:12-16), the assessed vow money (Lev. 27:2-8), and the offerings given freely by the people for Temple repair. Apparently, the priests were to live off of the tithes that the people were to bring for the care of the Levites (Num. 18:24). However, by the twenty-third year of Jehoash's reign, the priests had not repaired the Temple. Accordingly, Jehoash took the repair of the Temple and its financing out of the hands of all of the priests (12:6-8). The alternate plan called for all of the offerings—probably excluding the tithes—to be placed by the people in a chest and used to pay the craftsmen for their labors (12:9-15). The priests were allowed to keep for their own use the guilt and sin offerings, which were required by the trespasses of the people (12:16). Jehoash's vassalage to Hazael, the king of Syria, came after Jehoiada's death and because of Jehoash's sin (12:17-18; 2 Chron. 24:15,17,23).

The Reigns of Jehoahaz and His Son Jehoash of Israel (13:1-25)

The wicked reign of Jehoahaz (vv. 1-9).—Jehoahaz, the son of Jehu, plunged headlong after his father in calf worship and its attendant evils (v. 2). The deeper the nation of Israel went in sin the more severely God pressed upon them his chastening hand. God had given the Transjordan area of the Promised Land to the Syrians under Hazael (10:32) and continued to use Hazael to chastize them severely (v. 3). Indeed, Hazael sorely vexed Israel throughout the seventeen years of Jehoahaz's reign (13:22). Jehoahaz finally cried out to the Lord for mercy when his army was pitifully reduced (vv. 4,7). Jehoahaz's destitution is seen in that he could muster only ten chariots, whereas Ahab provided two thousand chariots as his part of the Battle of Karkar (Qarqar). The "savior" (v. 5) the Lord raised up seemingly took the form of the son and grandson of Jehoahaz. Jehoash, his son, regained the cities taken from Jehoahaz by Hazael (13:25). Jeroboam II, the grandson of Jehoahaz, regained the

Transjordan area and extended the borders of Israel to the point of glory under Solomon (14:25,27; 1 Kings 8:65). In spite of God's mercy and grace, the people did not turn from the sin of calf worship. "Asherah" (v. 6) was the image of the female consort of Baal erected by Ahab (1 Kings 16:33) and apparently not destroyed by Jehu (10:27). We can only point to the problem of the chronology of verses 1 and 10 and express the conviction that we could reconcile the seeming discrepancy if we had all of the facts.

The wicked reign of Jehoash; the death of Elisha (vv. 10-25).—After a brief description of the wicked reign of Jehoash (vv. 10-13), attention is focused upon Elisha from whom Jehoash sought and received help for deliverance from the Syrian oppression (vv. 14-25).

The last reference to Elisha was more than forty years before in relation to the revolt of Jehu (9:1). Elisha, who had received from the Lord a double portion of Elijah's spirit, had proven himself even to the wicked king to be the real protector of Israel. With his exclamation "my father, my father" (v. 14), Jehoash expressed more than his veneration for Elisha. He asked Elisha to intercede for him and Israel that the power of God might bring deliverance. The arrow Elisha instructed Jehoash to shoot from the window toward the east symbolized the victory God would give Israel over Syria (vv. 15-17). Elisha laid his hands on the hands of the king to show that the power for the victory would come from God as mediated through the prophet. "Until you have made an end of them" (v. 17) expressed God's desire to use Jehoash to destroy completely Syria's hold on Israel. Jehoash had to implement the promised victory by his own military action. His striking the ground only three times indicated that he did not have the zeal to obtain the full available victory (vv. 18-19). The body placed hurriedly in the nearby tomb of Elisha could easily have touched the bones of the prophet (vv. 20-21). The restoration of the body to life symbolized that Elisha's prophetic powers lived on though he was dead. Accordingly, Elisha's last prophecy was fulfilled (vv. 24-25). "Until now" (v. 23) indicates that the writer and/or editor of Kings lived during the captivity.

The Reign of Amaziah of Judah (14:1-22)

Amaziah, like his father Jehoash, served God, but not with a perfect heart (v. 3; 2 Chron. 25:2). His sparing of the sons of his father's assassins was according to the law of Moses (v. 6; Deut. 24:16). However, the death of Jehoash, his father, was the result of his father's murder of the prophet Zechariah (2 Chron. 24:25). Accordingly, the whole series of killings would be judged as murders.

Edom revolted from Judah during the reign of Jehoram as part of God's punishment of that wicked king (2 Kings 8:20-22). Originally, Amaziah planned for his force to retake Edom to be strengthened by one hundred thousand mercenaries of Israel (2 Chron. 25:6). Amaziah, however, dismissed these at the prophet's insistence that including them would result in an unholy alliance that would spell defeat for Judah (2 Chron. 25:7-10). Sela (v. 7), the capital of the Edomites that Amaziah renamed Jokthe-el, is today called Petra.

The occasion for Amaziah's war with Jehoash of Israel was perhaps the pillage of the Judean villages by the returning mercenaries of Israel (v. 8; 2 Chron. 25:13). The analogy depicts the thornbush proudly presenting itself as the equal of the cedar and being trampled underfoot by the wild beast as punishment (vv. 9-10). Amaziah's defeat and humiliation at the hands of Jehoash of Israel resulted from Amaziah's bringing back to Jerusalem and worshiping the gods of the defeated Edomites (vv. 11-14; 2 Chron. 25:14-16,20). Amaziah's death at the hands of assassins was also occasioned by his turning away from the Lord (v. 19; 2 Chron. 25:27).

The Reign of Jeroboam II of Israel (14:23-29)

This short treatment of Jeroboam's reign shows the religious perspective from which the Kings material was written. Although Jeroboam II led Israel to a time of unprecedented prosperity (v. 25), only two small paragraphs are given to his forty-one year reign. Secular historians would call him great, but those who wrote from the prophetic viewpoint only called him wicked (v. 24). The political expansion and peace enjoyed during his reign came because God chose him to answer his grandfather's prayer for relief to oppressed Israel (vv. 25-27; 2 Kings 13:4-5). Jonah, the son of Amittai, who prophesied the God-given expansion that Israel would enjoy under Jeroboam II (v. 25), is known to us from the Book of Jonah. The moral bankruptcy of Israel during the reign of Jeroboam II can be seen in the Books of Amos and Hosea, other prophets who ministered during that time. Indeed, Amos likened the prosperity of Israel under Jeroboam II to a basket of overripe summer fruit doomed to speedy decay (Amos 8:1-2). Israel had left only a little over thirty-two years of anarchy before their captivity under the Assyrians would begin and a little over forty-one years before their complete end as a nation (15:29; 17:6).

The Reign of Azariah (Uzziah) of Judah (15:1-7)

Azariah, who is also called Uzziah (vv. 1,13), is generally thought of as a good king. His mother's name was Jecoliah (v. 2), which means "the Lord has prevailed." His names Azariah and Uzziah mean respectively "the Lord has helped" and "the Lord has strengthened." Both of these names point to some experience in which the Lord God of Israel gave some significant victory to the family of Uzziah that contributed to their faith in God. Uzziah, however, followed his father Amaziah in being only partially obedient to God (v. 3). Uzziah, who began his reign at the age of sixteen and reigned for fifty-two years (v. 2), was instructed in the fear of the Lord by Zechariah. Nothing is known about this Zechariah except that he "had understanding in the vision of God" (2 Chron. 26:5, KJV). God blessed Uzziah as long as Uzziah sought the Lord, and Uzziah became exceedingly strong and prosperous. Read 2 Chronicles 26:6-15 for details concerning his army and military victories, his accomplishment in building and husbandry, and his general fame. Uzziah, however, was untrue to God in his latter years. Particularly, he sought in his pride to usurp the role of the priest (2 Chron. 26:16). He perhaps wanted to be like heathen kings such as Ethbaal, the king of Sidon, who was both king and priest. He probably would not have been severely punished had he repented at the rebuke of Azariah the priest (2 Chron. 26:18-19). But when Uzziah in anger refused to repent, God smote him with leprosy for the remaining years of his life (v. 5). Two results of his leprosy are mentioned. One was his being made to dwell in "a separate house" (v. 5), which was probably a house away from the palace area where the king lived in isolation. His isolation also included exclusion from the house of God (2 Chron. 26:21). Second, his son Jotham became coregent, exercising dominion over the palace and performing the duties of governing the people (v. 5). Although the time of Uzziah's affliction with leprosy is not stated, it must have been in the latter years of his reign. His son Jotham, who began to reign as sole king at the age of twenty-five (2 Kings 15:33), assumed administrative responsibilities for the kingdom immediately upon his father's affliction, which would have required Jotham's being at the time at least in his older teens. The blight of leprosy continued on Uzziah even in his burial in that he was not buried in the royal tomb, but in a field belonging to the kings (v. 7; 2 Chron. 26:23). Before the end of Uzziah's reign, the prophets Amos, Hosea, and Isaiah had begun their active careers (Amos 1:1; Hosea 1:1; Isa. 1:1; 6:1). A well-remembered earthquake occurred during Uzziah's reign, which Amos used to date his prophecy and which Zechariah used to illustrate the cataclysmic events of the second coming of Christ (Amos 1:1; Zech 14:3-5).

The Reign of Zechariah of Israel: The Fall of the House of Jehu (15:8-12)

This passage completes the record concerning the taking of the kingdom from the house of Jehu. Zechariah, the son of Jeroboam II, was the fourth generation of the sons of Jehu to sit upon the throne of Israel. The name Zechariah, which means "the Lord remembers," was fitting for the last king of the house of Jehu. Not only did God remember to bring to pass his promise to cause four generations of the sons of Jehu to reign in his stead (v. 12; 10:30), but God also remembered to avenge the blood-guiltiness of Jehu for his ruthlessness in executing the house of Ahab and to cut off Jehu's house for their sin of calf worship. Ibleam, which is located north of Samaria and a little south of Jezreel, was the site where Jehu and his followers mortally wounded Ahaziah, the king of Judah (9:27). It was, accordingly, a fitting site for God's judgment to bring to an end the house of Jehu.

The Reigns of Shallum, Menahem, Pekahiah, and Pekah of Israel (15:13-31)

The record of the taking away of the kingdom from all of the seed of Israel now begins, and we see the rapid plunge of the nation of Israel to destruction at the hands of the Lord for their sin. Anarchy now characterized the nation. Of these four kings, only Menahem died a natural death. The others died at the hands of conspirators. Also, the nation of Assyria, under the leadership of Tiglath-pileser III, who assumed the name Pul, moved once again to dominate the Near East and to cast its long shadow across the nation of Israel. Before the reign of Pekah had ended, the Assyrians had swallowed up a large portion of the land of

Israel and had taken many of the Israelites captive (15:29).

The reign of Shallum (15:13-16).—Shallum, who killed Zechariah and usurped his throne, was himself killed and replaced by Menahem after a one month reign (vv. 13-14). The ascension of Menahem to the throne meant that four kings had reigned in Israel in less than a year. Menahem is thought to have been a commander in the army of King Zechariah and to have moved from his station at Tirzah to Samaria to avenge Zechariah's murder. Menahem probably punished Tappuah for loyalty to Shallum (v. 16). His atrocity in cutting open the wombs of women with child is without precedent among the kings of Israel and especially toward their brethren. Such action reflects the absolute blackness of Menahem's heart. However, all of this was part of the cruel fate the Israelites had brought upon themselves by their sin. Already they had experienced such atrocities at the hands of the Ammonites and of the Syrians (Amos 1:13; 2 Kings 8:12). Moreover, such atrocities would be brought upon them for their sins by the Assyrians as part of their final tragedy (Hos. 13:16).

The reign of Menahem; the Assyrian takeover (15:17-22).—Although his name means "comforter," Menahem brought no real help to the nation of Israel, which was on the verge of destruction. He reigned for ten years and continued the evil of the previous kings of Israel (vv. 17-18). When the king of Assyria, who was known in Assyrian records as Tiglath-pileser III, and in the Babylonian records as Paul, invaded Israel, Menahem yielded himself to him and paid him one thousand talents of silver to secure his tottering throne (v. 19). Menahem raised the money by a tax of fifty shekels (about thirty to thirty-five dollars) each upon the wealthy men of Israel (v. 20). Inasmuch as one talent equals three thousand shekels, sixty thousand men of means were necessary to pay off the king of Assyria. The fact that there were at least sixty thousand wealthy men in Israel points to the prosperity of that age. The Assyrian inscriptions of Tiglath-pileaser III verify Menahem of Samaria as one of his vassals. From a positive standpoint, the conquest of Israel by the Assyrians and later by the Babylonians, the Medo-Persians, the Greeks, and the Romans became the means of extending to all people of the world the knowledge of the Lord God of Israel, the one true God. Menahem was succeeded at his death by his son, Pekahiah (v. 22).

The reign of Pekahiah (15:23-26).—The name Pekahiah means "the Lord opened." It is amazing that the people continued to take names pointing to their devotion to the Lord God of Israel when their hearts were so far from him. Hosea, the prophet, made it clear that by this time

Ephraim—another name for Israel—had been forsaken of God and had lost the ability to repent. Notice, for example, Hosea 4:17 and 5:4.

Pekahiah reigned for two years before he was assassinated by his captain Pekah, the son of Remaliah (vv. 23-25). "The Citadel" (v. 25) in which the king was assassinated was an especially fortified part of the royal palace. Pekahiah apparently followed Menahem's policy of vassalage to Assyria, whereas Pekah and the fifty Gileadites who joined him in the conspiracy againet Pekahiah were probably pro-Syrian (vv. 25,37).

The reign of Pekah (15:27-31).—Pekah, who continued the evil of his predecessors, was anti-Assyrian. Indeed, he sought to form with Rezin the king of Syria and with Ahaz the king of Judah a coalition against Assyria. When Jotham and Ahaz the kings of Judah refused to align themselves with them, Pekah of Israel and Rezin of Damascus attacked Judah in what is commonly known as the Syro-Ephraimite invasion. This crisis on the part of Judah provided the background for the prophecies in Isaiah chapters 7—12. In the end, however, the coalition attempt backfired on Pekah. The Assyrians swept through the fortified cities north of the Sea of Galilee, conquered "Gilead," which refers most likely to the land east of the Jordan belonging to Reuben, Gad, and the half-tribe of Manasseh, and "Galilee," which included all the land of Naphtali (v. 29). Moreover, Hoshea, leader of a pro-Assyrian conspiracy, murdered Pekah and reigned in his stead (v. 30). Many commentators take exception to assigning to Pekah a twenty-year reign, with various suggestions as to how it should be shortened or extended to fit their chronological scheme (v. 27). The Assyrian conquest of the cities of Israel and their enslavement of the people of Israel reduced the nation of Israel to a shadow of its former glory.

The Reigns of Jotham and Ahaz of Judah (15:32 to 16:20)

Against the background of the imminent destruction of Israel, one wonders why Judah continued to have comparative stability and prosperity. The answer lies in the revivals of religion that came from time to time to Judah. Note, for example, the revival in Judah under King Asa and his son Jehoshaphat that brought the nation back to God after the wicked reigns of King Rehoboam and his son Abijam (1 Kings 15:9-24; 22:41-50; 2 Chron. 15:1-19; 17:1 to 21:1). In contrast, Israel never experienced a revival. Also, Israel never had a king who did right in the sight of God, whereas many kings of Judah were devoted to the Lord, if not with a perfect heart.

The reign of Jotham (15:32-38).—After an undetermined time of coregency with his leprous father Uzziah (2 Kings 15:5), Jotham became the sole ruler of Judah and reigned for sixteen years. The notation that Hoshea murdered Pekah "in the twentieth year of Jotham" (v. 30) views the reign of Jotham from the standpoint of the total years he spent on the throne, including his coregency. The name Jotham, which means "the Lord is perfect," has been found on an official seal in the excavation of Ezion-Geber. Jerusha, the mother of Jotham, was the daughter of Zadok, who may have been the priest whose lineage goes back to Eleazar, the son of Aaron (v. 33; 1 Chron. 24:3; 2 Sam. 8:17; 1 Kings 1:32).

Jotham, who was looked upon as a good king, was not perfect in his devotion to the Lord. His devotion to God is likened to that of his father, who in turn was likened to his father, and so forth. The line goes back to Jehoash and Amaziah, both of whom had glaring weaknesses in their faith (v. 34; 14:3; 15:3). Jotham, however, did not make the mistake of Uzziah in usurping priestly authority (2 Chron. 27:2). His weakness in devotion to the Lord resulted in the people's continuing to follow the corrupt practices of the worship of the Lord at the high places (v. 35; 2 Chron. 27:2). Nonetheless, Jotham was sufficiently devoted to God for the Lord to make him mighty (2 Chron. 27:6). "The upper gate of the house of the Lord" refers to the gate of the inner court of the Temple that faced north (v. 35; Ezek. 9:2). Sometimes this was referred to as "the altar gate" because there the sacrifices were slaughtered (Ezek. 40:38-39). "Built" means to restore and/or to beautify. Other building projects of Jothan included the fortification of Ophel and of cities in the hill country of Judah (2 Chron. 27:3-4). He also subdued and extracted tribute from the Ammonites (2 Chron. 27:5). In short, it could be said that Jotham continued the work of his father Uzziah in providing security and prosperity for his people.

Not everything was well, however. The Syrians, who had been subjugated by Jeroboam II (14:28) and later by the Assyrians, took advantage of a lapse of Assyrian domination in the area to stop paying tribute to Assyria and to organize an anit-Assyrian alliance. Initially, Syria sought to include both Israel and Judah in the alliance, but when Jotham refused to be part of the alliance Syria and Israel decided to fight with Judah to force them into the alliance. "In those days" (v. 37) is to be interpreted to mean that Syria and Israel began to make their move against Jotham in the last days of Jotham, but did not appear before Jerusalem until the very beginning of the reign of Ahaz. "The Lord began to send" (v. 37) is to be interpreted as God's causing this invasion to come to test what Jotham and Ahaz would do. Whereas Jotham seemed disposed to trust the Lord, Isaiah 7—9 indicates that Ahaz spurned the offered help of the Lord and turned for security to an alliance with Assyria.

The reign of Ahaz (16:1-20).—Ahaz was a thoroughly wicked king. Three specific descriptions of his sin are given. First, "he walked in the ways of the kings of Israel" (v. 3a). Reference is both to the idolatrous and licentious practices of calf worship and to the worship of Baal, the fertility cult (2 Chron. 28:2). Second, he reintroduced the abominable practice of child sacrifice, which Solomon in his apostasy had first brought into Israel's life (v. 3b; 1 Kings 11:5-7). Perhaps Ahaz's sin of rejecting God's offer of help led Ahaz in desperation to sacrifice even his own son to heathen gods in hope of obtaining deliverance. "Whom the Lord drove out before the people of Israel" (v. 3c) implied God's judgment upon such abominable practices. Third, he himself violated God's command to worship only the Lord God of Israel at the prescribed place in the prescribed manner (v. 4; Deut. 12:2).

"Then" (v. 5) indicates that Ahaz's sin brought judgment in the form of the Syro-Ephraimite invasion. Although Ahaz spurned God's gracious offer to help, God did not allow the invaders to take the city Jerusalem. Judah did, however, suffer terribly at the hands of the invaders. In addition to spoiling Judah, the invaders killed in one day one hundred and twenty thousand of Judah's soldiers, led captive two hundred thousand men, women, and children of Judah, and killed the son of Ahaz (2 Chron. 28:6-8). Also, Ahaz's sin resulted in the rebellion of the Edomites, who regained their dominion over the Gulf of Aqaba, and the invasion of the Philistines, who captured strategic cities of Judah (v. 6; 2 Chron. 28:17-19).

Isaiah the prophet strongly encouraged Ahaz to turn to the Lord for help and even promised to bring to pass any requested sign to prove that God would indeed deliver Judah from the hands of the kings of Syria and of Israel (Isa. 7:1-11). Ahaz, however, piously refused God's help and paid Tiglath-pileaser III with gold and silver to help (vv. 7-9; Isa. 7:12). Isaiah then gave Ahaz the sign of the virgin who would bring forth a child and predicted that the Assyrians to whom Ahaz had turned would become the scourge of God upon wicked Judah (Isa. 7:13-17). Although the sign had immediate application to Ahaz, its long-term fulfillment meant a cutting off of the faithless line of David through Solomon so that the Messiah came from the seed of David through the line of Nathan. See commentary on 2 Chronicles 7:1-22.

Ahaz turned in his distress and spiritual blindness more and more away from the Lord (2 Chron. 28:22). While on a trip to Damascus to pay homage to Tiglath-pileser III for his deliverance, he saw and had made for himself an altar to the gods of Damascus (vv. 10-11). His thought was that the Syrian gods had demonstrated their superiority to the Lord God of Israel and that he would worship them (2 Chron. 28:23). Accordingly, he replaced the bronze altar of the Lord with the Syrian altar and commanded that all the sacrifices be offered upon it (vv. 12-15). Note that the Syrian altar of Ahaz is called "his altar" (v. 14) in contrast with the Lord's altar. "To inquire by" (v. 15) may mean that Ahaz used the replaced altar of the Lord for seeking revelation by examining the entrails of sacred animals, a practice common among the Assyrians and the Babylonians. Ahaz further desecrated the house of God by mutilating the holy vessels to pay tribute to Tiglath-pileser (vv. 17-18). He even shut the doors to the house of God, thereby suspending Temple worship (2 Chron. 28:24).

The Reign of Hoshea: The End of Israel (17:1-41)

This long passage describes the end of Israel (vv. 1-6), the sins for which Israel fell and for which Judah would ultimately fall (vv. 7-23), and finally the Assyrian resettlement of the land of Israel (vv. 24-41).

The end of Israel (vv. 1-6).—The Northern Kingdom fell to the Assyrians in the ninth year of Hoshea's reign, which was approximately 722 BC. Although Hoshea himself, whose name means "salvation," was the least wicked of all of the kings of Israel (v. 2), the cup of Israel's iniquity had been filling up for centuries and now stood overflowing. Hoshea, who led a pro-Assyrian conspiracy to kill Pekah and usurp his throne, rebelled against Assyria. He turned for help to Egypt, the great rival of Assyria for world domination (vv. 3-4). The king of Assyria immediately arrested Hoshea, invaded the land of Israel, and captured Samaria after a three-year siege (vv. 5-6). "Shalmaneser king of Assyria" (v. 3) refers to Shalmaneser V (727-722 BC), the son and successor of Tiglath-pileser III. Shalmaneser V apparently began the siege of Samaria, but died before Samaria fell. Sargon II (722-703 BC), the brother of Shalmaneser V, actually conquered Samaria in his accession year and carried a large number of the people of Israel into captivity. "Halah" (v. 6) is thought to be a district in the Assyrian Empire through which the Habor River flows. "Gozan" (v. 6) is a town located on the Habor River.

"The cities of the Medes" (v. 6) would be located in the area east of the Tigris River. The Israelites transported to Assyria apparently settled down there and eventually assimilated themselves among the people. Sargon II numbered those taken captive from the city of Samaria as 27,290, a surprisingly small number. We must, however, remember that others were taken captive earlier. In either case, the Northern Kingdom was taken away, never to be heard of again.

Sins for which Israel was carried away (vv. 7-23).—The keys to interpretating this passage are the words "because" (v. 7), "yet" (v. 13), "but" (v. 14), and "therefore" (v. 18). Captivity came "because the people of Israel had sinned against the Lord their God" (v. 7a). Their sins range all the way from ingratitude to the Lord God of Israel, who brought them out of the bondage of Egypt and established them in the Promised Land, to the idolatrous and licentious worship of the Lord under the figure of golden calves, to the abominable practices that caused God to drive the Canaanites out of the land (vv. 7b-12). However, the concluding summary (vv. 21-23) points to the failure of the people to reject the calf worship introduced by Jeroboam as the basic reason for the fall of northern Israel. Had they purified themselves of this distorted worship of the Lord God of Israel, they would have found the moral strength to reject the wicked practices of the Canaanites.

"Yet the Lord warned" (v. 13) points to God who in mercy withheld from them their deserved punishment and who in grace reached out to warn them through his prophets from the way of destruction into the path of peace. "But they would not listen, but were stubborn" (v. 14) denotes their abuse of God's mercy and grace. With the same stubbornness that characterized their fathers, they "despised his statutes, and his covenant . . . and the warnings which he gave them (v. 15). "Despised," which means basically to reject, was rooted in their contempt for God and his ways. In despising God, they plunged deeper and deeper into sin (vv. 15b-17). "Became false" (v. 15b) means that the Israelites became empty and vain just like the "false idols" they worshiped. People indeed do become like the gods or the God they worship.

"Therefore the Lord was very angry with Israel, and removed them out of his sight" (v. 18) points to the consequence of their willful, malicious, and persistent sin. "Very" in the expression "very angry" (v. 18) has as its basic idea to grow and grow to exceeding and overwhelming magnitude. The people continued to abuse the longsuffering of God and to excite his anger with their sins until he finally removed them forever as a nation. Only Judah remained of the twelve tribes of Israel to whom God had given the Promised Land. However, the editor of the Books of Kings, who lived after the destruction of Jerusalem, anticipated in verses 19-20 the rejection of all Israel, including Judah, for their sin.

Resettlement of Israel: the people and their religion (vv. 24-41).—After some lapse of time, "the king of Assyria" (v. 24), who was by then Esarhaddon, resettled the land of Israel with people from the eastern portion of his empire (v. 24; Ezra 4:2). Perhaps they also were conquered people whom Esarhaddon dispossessed from their original home. These settled in the Land and intermarried with the Israelites who remained there. Thereafter, the people of that area were known as Samaritans.

When those transplanted in Israel first came into the Land, they did not regard the Lord God of Israel (v. 25a). But when God caused lions that had multiplied in the dormant land to devour some of them, they pled with the king of Assyria to send a priest of Israel to teach them how to worship the god of the Land (vv. 25b-26). The priest who instructed them worshiped the Lord after the idolatrous and licentious practices of calf worship (vv. 27-28). Their final worship style was a combination of fearing the Lord and serving their own gods (vv. 29-33). They offered sacrifices to the Lord to appease him as the god of the Land, while following the heathen practices of their ancestors. In comparing their worship with what was required by God of his people, their religion was false: "they do not fear the Lord" (v. 34b). Their mongrel religion was the basis of the continued rejection of the Samaritans by the Jews to and beyond the writing of the Books of Kings (vv. 34-41; Ezra 4:3).

The Kingdom of Judah from the Fall of Israel to the Babylonian Captivity
2 Kings 18:1 to 25:30

Judah now stood alone! The virgin of Israel had fallen, the victim of her apostasy against her God (Amos 5:2). Judah's days also were limited. Indeed, the sad theme of these chapters is the taking of the kingdom from Judah. In another one hundred and thirty years, Judah would be swept completely away into the Babylonian captivity because of her sin against God.

The godly reign of Hezekiah, who ruled under the tutelage of Isaiah the prophet, brought fleeting hope for the salvation of Judah. But the unprecedented wickedness of Manassah's reign caused Judah to cross the line of God's mercy and thereafter be marked for destruction. After the reign of Manasseh, the only question was when Judah would be destroyed. Even repentance by Manasseh in his later years and the reforms of godly King Josiah could not avert their plunge to destruction. After deportations in 605 BC and 597 BC, the end finally came in 587 BC with the fall of Jerusalem after the combined wicked reigns of Jehoahaz, Jehoiakim, Jehoiachin, and Zedekiah. The Book of 2 Kings concludes with the record of Evil-merodach's gracious care of Jehoiachin, which provided a prelude of good yet to come to the people of God in fulfillment of his promise to David "to establish the throne of his kingdom for ever" (2 Sam. 7:13).

The Reign of Hezekiah (18:1 to 20:21)

The lengthy discussion in the Kings materials of the reign of Hezekiah is due to Hezekiah's close association with Isaiah the prophet. As such, the record is comparable to the lengthy emphasis given to the reign of Ahab because of his association with Elijah and Elisha. Note that 2 Kings 18:13 to 20:19 is reproduced almost verbatim in Isaiah 36—39. Other prophets contemporary with Hezekiah are Hosea in the Northern Kingdom and Micah in the Southern Kingdom (Hos. 1:1; Mic. 1:1).

The Length and Character of His Reign (18:1-8)

Hezekiah, who came to the throne at the age of twenty-five and reigned for twenty-nine years, was totally dedicated to the Lord God of Israel (vv. 1-3). "All" (v. 3) indicates that he even matched his godly ancestor David in devotion to the Lord. His mother's name was "Abi," meaning "my father," or "Abijah," meaning "my father is the Lord" (v. 2; 2 Chron. 29:1). The mention of her father "Zechariah" (v. 2), which means "the Lord remembers," suggests that Hezekiah's mother came from a prominent family who were probably distinguished by their devotion to God.

Hezekiah, whose name means "the Lord strengthens," took several remarkable steps in the first year of his reign to promote godliness in Judah. First, he reopened and repaired the doors of the house of the Lord, which had been closed by Ahaz his father (2 Chron. 29:3). Second, he led the Levites to sanctify themselves and the house of God and

to minister therein as God's servants (2 Chron. 29:14-19). Third, he restored worship in the house of God (2 Chron. 29:20-36). Fourth, he
reinstituted the Passover feast and the feast of Unleavened Bread and
invited the remnant of the northern tribes to join Judah in the observance of these feasts (2 Chron. 30:1-22). Fifth, he reunited the nation to
the Lord so that God heard their prayers for blessings (2 Chron.
30:23-27). Sixth, he moved with the enthusiastic support of the revived
priests and people to purge the land of idolatry (v. 4; 2 Chron. 31:1). For
the first time in the history of Judah, he removed the high places. (See
comment on 1 Kings 3:1-3.) Then he removed the pillars and images
related to the worship of Baal and his consort Asherah. (See comments
on 1 Kings 11:1-40; 16:29-34.) Finally, he destroyed the bronze serpent
of Moses that the people in the darkened minds of their apostasy had
worshiped as an idol. "Nehushtan," the name given by the people to the
serpent of Moses, means "bronze thing." Seventh, Hezekiah pressed
additional reforms to care for the priesthood and the house of God (2
Chron. 31:2-21).

In the area of personal trust in God, Hezekiah was superior to any
king of Judah before or after him (v. 5). The later reference to Josiah's
superiority is in relation to his adherence to the Mosaic law (2 Kings
23:25). "Trusted" (v. 5) has as its basic idea to cast one's self upon someone or something for security. The pro-Assyrian party, which was followed by Ahaz, Hezekiah's father, counseled alliances with Assyria for
security. The pro-Egyptian party saw the nation's security as being best
protected by alliances with Epypt. But Hezekiah—encouraged by Isaiah
particularly—put his hope and confidence in the Lord God of Israel. His
trust in God did not negate military preparation, but gave him wisdom
for fortifying his nation and organizing his army (2 Chron. 32:1-8).
Under the severest test, which would be illustrated in the Assyrian crisis,
Hezekiah adhered to the Lord and to his commandments, with one exception (v. 6,13-16). Accordingly, God was with Hezekiah and prospered his way (v. 7). As the result, Hezekiah was able to throw off the
yoke of Assyrian vassalage pressed upon Judah during the reign of Ahaz
his father (v. 7b). Also, he was able to chastise the Philistines for their
invasion of Judah during the days of his father and to regain from them
the cities which they had taken from his father (v. 8).

Hezekiah and the Assyrian Aggression (18:9 to 19:37)

Much like today, several nations vied for superiority in the Middle East
during the eighth century BC. Assyria to the east continued to be the

dominant military power. But Assyria was challenged from time to time by the emerging neo-Babylonian Empire, which finally conquered Niveveh, the capital of the Assyrian Empire, in 612 BC. Also, Egypt to the south periodically flexed her muscles and pressed northward in hope of attaining her former glory. Political intrigue was the order of the day.

The fall of Samaria (18:9-12).—This section is essentially a summary of the previous account of the fall of Samaria and the deportation of the Israelites (17:5-23). The significant additional matter is that the siege and conquest of Samaria is related respectively to the fourth and sixth years of the reign of Hezekiah. Accordingly, the stage is set to show how Hezekiah handled the Assyrian aggression, which swept away Israel.

Hezekiah's submission to Assyrian vassalage (18:13-16).—Hezekiah had refused to pay tribute to Assyria as his father Ahaz had done (v. 14; 16:8). In time, Sennacherib, who succeeded Sargon as king of Assyria, stormed into Judah to punish the rebellious Hezekiah and took all of Judah's fortified cities except Jerusalem (v. 13). Lachish, which at the time was under siege, ultimately fell, as is pictured in the famous relief on the wall of Sennacherib's palace in Nineveh. According to the famous Taylor Prism, Sennacherib claimed to have Hezekiah shut up like a bird in a cage.

"The fourteenth year" indicates that this invasion occurred either shortly before or after Hezekiah's illness and miraculous recovery (18:2; 20:6). Indeed, Hezekiah's illness may have been God's chastisement upon Hezekiah for his lack of faith in surrendering to the king of Assyria. In any case, Hezekiah weakened momentarily in his faith and sent peace envoys to the king of Assyria at Lachish. He confessed repentance of his rebellion against Assyria and paid the enormous demand of three hundred talents of silver and thirty talents of gold (vv. 14-15). The Babylonian talent, which was probably the standard measure of weight for Palestine, was 30.13 kilograms or 66.29 pounds. To meet the Assyrian demand, Hezekiah not only gave Sennacherib all of the silver in the treasuries of the Temple and of the palace, but stripped off and gave to him the gold plates with which Hezekiah had overlaid the Temple doors and doorposts (vv. 15-16; 2 Chron. 29:3).

Hezekiah's refusal to submit to further demands of Assyria (18:17 to 19:37).—Although Sennacherib took the tribute money, he did not depart as promised. Rather, he sent a large army against Jerusalem under three Assyrian officials to demand Hezekiah's unconditional surrender. Apparently, their design was to deport the Judahites as they had the Israelites (18:31-32). "Tartan" is the title for the commander-in-chief of the Assyrian army. "Rabsaris" means chief eunuch. He was the personal servant of the king. "Rabshakeh" means chief cupbearer. His work often involved administrative affairs. The Rabshakeh, probably because of his linguistic and diplomatic abilities, led the discussion with the officials of Hezekiah and perhaps the expedition (18:19,26-28,37; 19:8). These officials took up their position with their army at the upper conduit of the Gihon, which originally took the water of the gushing spring south along the highway of the Fuller's Field to the lower pool (v. 17b). However, Hezekiah, as part of his defense against the Assyrian aggression, had by this time extended the wall of the city to embrace the lower pool, had sealed up the outer entrance to Gihon, and had redirected its waters to the Pool of Siloam inside the walled city by his famous tunnel (20:20; 2 Chron. 32:1-8,30). In keeping with the status of these Assyrian officials, Hezekiah himself did not go out to meet them, but sent three of his chief officials to announce his refusal to capitulate (v. 18).

The Rabshakeh sought by his loud boasting to show Hezekiah and the people of Jerusalem the futility of their resistance (vv. 19-25). Particularly, he sought to undercut every ground of their hope for security against the Assyrians. First, he used the analogy of Egypt as a weak and harmful reed to show the folly of depending on Egyptian alliances for security (v. 21). Second, he sought to undercut Hezekiah's admonition that they should rely on the Lord for their security by suggesting that Hezekiah had offended the Lord God of Israel by tearing down his high places and restricting worship to the Temple in Jerusalem (v. 22). Third, he sought to undermine reliance on Judah's military might by showing the inability of Judah to match the military might of even one Assyrian captain (vv. 23-24). The Rabshakeh concluded his argument for surrender by agreeing with those who believed that Judah was doomed by God because of her sin and that Assyria was the rod of God's destruction against Judah as well as against Israel (v. 25).

The Judaean officials feared that the people would be influenced to surrender by the Rabshakeh's loud boasting and asked for the conversation to be carried on in Aramaic instead of Hebrew. But the Rabshakeh rejected their proposal and made a special appeal to the people to surrender (18:26-35). In particular, the Rabshakeh ridiculed the ability of the Lord God of Israel in whom Hezekiah was trusting to withstand the gods and the army of the Assyrians. Hamath and Arpad were cities on the northern border of Israel that fell to Assyria. Sepharvaim, Hena, and Ivvah (Avva) were Babylonian or Syrian cities conquered by the Assyrians from which the Assyrians brought colonists to repopulate north-

ern Israel (2 Kings 17:24). The people of Judah repudiated the Rabshakeh's appeal for surrender by their silence, and the chief officials of Judah
with clothes rent reported to Hezekiah the demands of the Assyrians (vv.
36-37).

Hezekiah humbled himself before God, went to the house of God for
prayer, and appealed to Isaiah the prophet for help (19:1-5). Hezekiah's
message to Isaiah involved a description of their terrible plight, his hope
that the Lord God of Israel had heard and would rebuke the blasph-
emous words of the Rabshakeh, and his appeal for Isaiah to beseech
God to save those of the people of God who had not yet been consumed
by the Assyrians. His analogy concerning the woman in travail denoted
both extreme danger and opportunity. On the one hand, lack of strength
to give birth would result in the probable death of both the mother and
the child. On the other hand, strength to give birth would result in safety
and joy for both the mother and child. With this analogy, Hezekiah
hinted at spiritual rebirth of the nation that could come from God's
deliverance of them.

Isaiah responded with a sure promise. The king of Assyria would hear
a rumor that would cause Sennacherib to return to his own land, and
there he would be killed with the sword (19:6-7). "Spirit" (v. 7) is another
example of God's sovereign control of everything, even evil spirits, to
work his will. See comments on 1 Kings 22:1-40.

Isaiah's prophecy was swiftly fulfilled (19:9-37). The Rabshakeh left
Jerusalem under siege and returned to Sennacherib, who by this time
was in siege against Libnah (v. 8). Sennacherib, upon hearing the rumor
that Tirhakah the king of Ethiopia had set out to fight against him, sent
a letter to Hezekiah making one last appeal for surrender (vv. 9-13).
Hezekiah once again turned to the Lord for help spreading the letter
before the Lord in the house of God and beseeching God to save Judah to
show all men that he alone is God (vv. 14-19). While Hezekiah prayed,
Isaiah received a divine revelation repeating and expanding the prediction of victory (vv. 20-34). The divine revelation contained a judgment
poem against Assyria (vv. 29-31) and a promise that Sennacherib would
return empty-handed to his own land without even coming to or shooting an arrow against Jerusalem, the city that God himself would defend
for his own honor and for the sake of his promises to David (vv. 32-34).
The same night of Hezekiah's prayer the judgment of God fell on the Assyrians. The miraculous death of 185,000 Assyrian soldiers may have
been caused by a plague. However, the implication is that they died
mysteriously in the night much like the firstborn sons of the Egyptians

(v. 35). This divine judgment caused Sennacherib to retreat without delay to Nineveh, where he was assassinated some time later in fulfillment of Isaiah's prophecy (vv. 36-37).

Hezekiah's Sickness and Recovery (20:1-11)

"In those days" (v. 1) is a general expression denoting sometime during, before, or after the Assyrian crisis. As has been noted, the extension of Hezekiah's life by fifteen years and his total reign of twenty-nine years means that his sickness came in about his fourteenth year. The ominous announcement of his death by Isaiah (v. 1) suggests that Hezekiah's illness was due to some breach of faith such as paying tribute to the Assyrians instead of standing in his God-given freedom. Had Hezekiah died at that time his line would probably have been cut off, for he was most likely without a son in his fourteenth year of reign, since Manasseh his son and successor began his reign at the age of twelve years.

Hezekiah's problem was a boil (v. 7), perhaps on or close to his head, with attendant blood poisoning. Hezekiah's prayers were effectual, and the prophet Isaiah, who had delivered the death oracle, was turned back to announce his complete healing within three days (vv. 2-6). Along with the announcement of an additional fifteen years of life for Hezekiah, Isaiah proclaimed that God would deliver Hezekiah and the city of Jerusalem out of the hands of the besieging Assyrians. His healing and God's promise of deliverance doubtless strengthened Hezekiah to withstand the pressure of the Assyrians to surrender. A poutice of compressed figs was a well-known remedy among the ancients for softening and opening boils.

Hezekiah's request for a sign may have been due to his fear that Isaiah's judgment oracle—once spoken—could not be reversed (v. 8). Accordingly, God turned back the shadow on the sundial to assure Hezekiah that the death oracle had been removed (vv. 9-11). A "sign" is an event, usually supernatural, by which a word from God is confirmed. "The dial of Ahaz" is literally "the steps of Ahaz." Accordingly, some interpret Ahaz's time-telling device to be the steps of an astral shrine. The sundial, which is the oldest known instrument for telling time, was invented by the Babylonians and probably came to Ahaz through the Assyrians. In a 360° dial, 10° represents forty minutes. How God performed the miracle of turning back the shadow on the dial we are not told. Obviously, God could have done it a number of ways. Some think that God moved the earth and the entire system that moves about the sun backward. That certainly is possible. Moreover, God who created the universe is capable of reversing it without destroying the machinery of the earth, of our solar system, or of the entire universe. The miracle could have been performed without turning back the solar system. For example, God could have miraculously altered the normal refraction of the rays of the sun so that it could be said that "the sun [the rays of the sun] turned back on the dial the ten steps by which it had declined" (Isa. 38:8).

Babylonian Overtures Toward Judah: Isaiah's Prediction of Babylonian Captivity (20:12-19)

"At that time" does not necessarily mean immediately following, but sometimes during the period after Hezekiah's miraculous recovery. The purpose for which Merodach-baladan, king of Babylon, sent his envoys was to congratulate Hezekiah on his recovery and to inquire about the turning back of the shadow on the sundial (v. 12; 2 Chron. 32:31). Another reason doubtless was to solicit Hezekiah's friendship for future revolts against the king of Assyria. Their coming was later interpreted as allowed by God to determine what was in Hezekiah's heart (2 Chron. 32:31). Hezekiah, flattered by the overtures of Babylon, foolishly revealed all the wealth of Israel to the Babylonian embassy (vv. 13-15). Isaiah then predicted the carrying away to Babylon of Judah's wealth and royal family (vv. 16-18). Hezekiah's response to Isaiah's prophecy is puzzling (v. 19). Did he interpret the coming captivity as good in itself or as working good in the life of God's people? Also, did he imply with his words "Why not, if there will be peace and security in my days?" that he didn't care about the future as long as there was peace and security in his day? Perhaps he meant to acknowledge the goodness of God in not bringing upon Judah in his lifetime their deserved punishment.

Concluding Observations Concerning His Reign (20:20-21)

The more than 500-yard long tunnel by which Hezekiah directed the waters of the Gihon into the city of Jerusalem for the sake of security against the Assyrians can be seen today in Jerusalem. Indeed, I had the privilege of going through it both in 1963 and again in 1973. An inscription in eighth century BC Hebrew, which was discovered on the wall of the tunnel in 1880, told how Hezekiah's laborers worked simultaneously from both ends and met in the middle. The inscription is now in the Istanbul museum.

The Reigns of Manasseh and Amon (21:1-26)

The Reign of Manasseh (21:1-18)

His apostasy (vv. 1-9).—After a brief notation of preliminary data, this passage describes the terrible apostasy of Manasseh that marked Judah irrevocably for destruction. Manasseh's reign of fifty-five years was the longest of any of Judah's kings. Hephzibah, his mother's name, means "my delight is in her," a name which Isaiah predicted God would ultimately give to restored and redeemed Zion (Isa. 62:4). But for the time being the Land was about to be plunged under the terrible judgment of God. Accordingly, Isaiah noted that Azubah and Shemamah, meaning respectively "Forsaken" and "Desolate," were fitting names for now (Isa. 62:4).

Manasseh means "he causes to forget." Hezekiah and Hephzibah may have so named their son because he brought consolation to them for the loss of an earlier child or perhaps because Hephzibah's joy in her son caused her to forget the pain of giving birth to him. In actuality, by his apostasy Manasseh caused the people of Judah to forget the godly influence of his father Hezekiah and even caused the people to be forgotten by God.

Manasseh's evil may have been to some degree fostered by his falling in the early years of his reign as a child under the influence of anti-prophetic parties who doubtless chafed under the godly reforms of his father Hezekiah. In his evil, Manasseh followed "the abominable practices of the nations whom the Lord drove out before the people of Israel" (v. 2). However, Manasseh's sin was "More wicked" (v. 11) because he sinned in spite of his greater knowledge of God, used his high position to corrupt the people of God, and corrupted Temple worship that was to reflect the true character of God. Specific sins mentioned are: (1) his rebuilding the high places his father Hezekiah had destroyed (v. 3a); (2) his following the ways of Ahab, king of Israel, in erecting altars to Baal and in making an image to Asherah, the consort of Baal (v. 3b); (3) his worshiping and serving the host of the heavens after the pattern of the Assyrians and King Ahaz (v. 3c); (4) his building altars for the worship of pagan deities in the house of the Lord and in the two courts thereof (vv. 4-5); (5) his burning his son(s) as an offering in the Valley of Hinnom (vv. 6a; 2 Chron. 33:6); (6) his practicing soothsaying and augury and consorting with mediums and with wizards (v. 6b); and (7) in his further defaming God by setting a graven image of Asherah in the house of God (vv. 7-8).

The result of his apostasy: the destruction of Judah (vv. 10-15).—The coming desolation of Judah and Jerusalem for Manasseh's sin was announced by the prophets (vv. 10-15). Prominent among these were Isaiah, Micah, Habakkuk, Zephaniah, Jeremiah, and Ezekiel. "The measuring line of Samaria" and "the plummet of the house of Ahab" are building analogies that obviously stand for the judgment of God to come upon Judah just as it had come upon Samaria and upon the house of Ahab. Judah had been measured by God, found crooked, and would be destroyed, just as Samaria and the house of Ahab had been destroyed. The wiping clean of the dish that had been used and then turning it over so as not to use it again represented the completeness of Judah's destruction. However, since the dish was not broken in pieces, the possibility of God's using them again was left open.

The critical issue was how God could forsake Jerusalem and remove the house of David from ruling in that city in view of God's repeated promise to establish forever David's house and his kingdom and to give him forever a lamp in Jerusalem. (See, for example, 2 Sam. 7:16; 22:17; 1 Kings 11:36; 15:4.) The answer is that God's promises to David and to the people of Israel were conditioned on their obedience to God (v. 9). In their repeatedly refusing to hear God's plea to them to turn from their sin and in their allowing themselves to be seduced by Manasseh, they brought about their own desolation. But God's promise to David was more than conditional: it was also sure. Accordingly, God would find a way in spite of their sinful natures to establish forever the kingdom of David and to make those of the nation of Israel his very own people who would serve as a kingdom of priests and would become a holy nation. The Kings material does not deal with how God would yet redeem Israel. The prophets, however, underscored that God in his steadfast and righteous love would find a way. Isaiah declared that God would redeem Israel through the ministry of the Suffering Servant who would give himself as an offering for their sin (Isa. 53:4-12).

His persecution of the innocent (v. 16).—Another reason for the desolation of Judah was the innocent blood shed by Manasseh. Numbered among these doubtless were many prophets. Indeed, early Christian tradition told of Manasseh's having Isaiah the prophet sawn in two by a wood saw.

Concluding observations (vv. 17-18).—"The Book of the Chronicles of the Kings of Judah," which is reflected in 2 Chronicles, provided additional information concerning the reign of Manasseh. Of particular interest is the Lord's causing Manasseh to be carried into captivity in Baby-

lon by the king of Assyria. Manasseh repented of his sins, was restored to
Jerusalem as King, and even instituted godly reforms (2 Chron.
33:11-16). Although Manasseh personally repented and lived thereafter
for God, he could not change the evil tide he had unleashed. In spite of
his efforts to turn the people back to God, they continued to worship in
the places of abomination. Initially, their worship was of the Lord on
pagan altars. Soon they forsook the Lord and gave themselves wholly
over to evil worship (2 Chron. 33:17).

The reign of Amon (vv. 19-26).—Amon continued the apostasy of his
father. However, he did not humble himself before God as Manasseh did
(2 Chron. 33:23). Conceivably, he intended to turn to God later on, but
he never had a chance. He was assassinated the second year of his reign
at the age of twenty-four.

The Reign of Josiah (22:1 to 23:30)

His Undeviating Devotion to the Lord (22:1-2)

Josiah, who ascended the throne at the age of eight and reigned
thirty-one years, was a wholehearted servant of the Lord God of Israel.
Indeed, he, along with his great-grandfather Hezekiah, stood head and
shoulders above the other kings of Judah in devotion to God, inasmuch
as they walked in "all the way of David" their father without departing
therefrom (v. 2; 23:25; 18:5-6). The later record indicates that Josiah
began "to seek the God of David his father" in the eighth year of his reign
when he was sixteen years of age (2 Chron. 34:3*a*). Then in the twelfth
year of his reign when he was twenty years old he began to purge Judah
and Jerusalem of their idolatrous practices and even extended his efforts
to purify the religion of the people of God to Simeon, Manasseh,
Ephraim, and as far north as Naphtali (2 Chron. 34:3*b*-7). The mention of Josiah's mother and his grandmother suggest that they probably
had a great deal to do with his devotion to the Lord (v. 1).

His Great Reformation (22:3 to 23:27)

*His repair of the Temple and discovery of the Book of the Law
(22:3-8).*—Josiah began his greatest work as a religious reformer when
he was twenty-six years of age by repairing the house of the Lord, which
led to the discovery of the book of the law. The Temple had been neglected and defiled furing the fifty-seven years of the wicked reigns of
Manasseh and his son Amon. Apparently, Josiah had reinstated the

plan used to repair the Temple in the reign of Jehoash. (See comments on 2 Kings 11:21 to 12:21.) "The book of the law" discovered was at least the Book of Deuteronomy and conceivably the whole of the Pentateuch, since those five books are unusually designated "the book of the law" (2 Chron. 17:9; Ezra 6:18; Neh. 8:1; 9:3; 13:1).

The effect on Josiah of the reading of the book of the law (22:9-14). — Shaphan probably did not read all of the book of the law to the king. He doubtless did read to him the blessing and curses that would come upon those who kept or failed to keep the law of God (Deut. 28; Lev. 26). Alarmed at the words of the book concerning their sins, Josiah humbled himself before God and immediately sent to inquire of Huldah the prophetess as to the fate of himself, his people, and his nation for the transgression of their fathers of the laws of God.

Huldah's prophetic word concerning Judah and Josiah (22:15-20). — Huldah's prophetic reply was in two parts. On the one hand, Judah would indeed experience for its transgressions all the desolation and curses described in Deuteronomy 28 and Leviticus 26 (vv. 15-17). On the other hand, God would not destroy Judah and Jerusalem in Josiah's day, because Josiah had repented and humbled himself before God in hearing of God's judgment upon their sin (vv. 18-20). "Peace" (v. 20) meant that Josiah would not experience the desolation and does not rule out his dying in battle.

Public reading of the book of the law and the making of the covenant (23:1-3). —Rather than content himself with the promise that the nation would be spared desolation in his day, Josiah sought the return of the whole nation to God by leading them into a covenant with the Lord based on the book of the law. "The elders of Judah" (v. 1) represented all the people of Judah. With them, the priests, and the prophets, Josiah assembled "all the people, both small and great," that is, the common citizens as well as the rich and prominent. "The book of the covenant" (v. 2) seemingly is another expression for the book of the law, which had been discovered in the Temple. "The pillar" (v. 3) was either Jachin or Boaz, which was the place designated for the king to stand in worship before God and the people (1 Kings 7:21; 2 Kings 11:14). "Joined in" (v. 3) means "take one's stand." The people perhaps sat while the king read and then stood to indicate their commitment to join Josiah in the covenant with the Lord. See comments on 2 Kings 11:17-20 for an interpretation of the covenant into which they entered.

Reforms in Jerusalem and Judah and outside Judah (23:4-20). —Josiah now intensified his effort to eradicate idolatry and all pagan practices from the life of the people of God. Verses 4-14 describe his reforms in Jerusalem and in Judah, and verses 15-20 describes determination of idolatry in Bethel and all other cities of Samaria. His destruction of the golden calf altar at Bethel, his execution of the pagan priests, and his burning upon the golden calf altar the bones of pagan priests there buried were actions by which Josiah fulfilled the prophecy of the man of God out of Judah concerning him (1 Kings 13:1-2). The ability of Josiah to press his reforms in the North illustrates the waning power of Assyria during his reign.

Celebration of the Passover in Jerusalem (23:21-23).—Josiah climaxed his reforms during his eighteenth year with the celebration of the Passover at the house of God in Jerusalem according to the law of Moses (Deut. 16:1-8). In previous observances of the Passover, insufficient attention had been given to details. For example, the great Passover of Hezekiah was observed in the second month instead of the prescribed first month and without proper purification of some of the people (2 Chron. 30:2-3,17-20). Josiah's observance was distinguished in absolute adherence to all Mosaic laws.

Further reformation and praise of Josiah (23:24-25).—Josiah and his great-grandfather Hezekiah both receive the acclaim of being the most devout kings in the history of Judah. As had been noted, Hezekiah was especially distinguished in his absolute confidence in God even under great duress and Josiah in his absolute adherence to the laws of Moses.

Failure of Josiah and his reformation to save Judah (23:26-27).—"Still" (v. 26), which means "howbeit, yet, but," contrasts this paragraph with the personal godliness and reforms of Josiah just described. In spite of Josiah's sincere conversion, his personal adherence to the laws of God, and his extermination of outward idolatry, he could not save the nation of Judah and the city of Jerusalem from God's judgment upon them for their sin, which had reached the point of no return under Manasseh's wicked influence. See comments on 2 Kings 23:31-35 to see how the people reflected their deep-seated wickedness in reverting at Josiah's death to the evil practices of Manasseh and Amon and the other wicked kings of Judah.

Concluding Observations Concerning Josiah's Reign (23:28-30)

Although good ultimately brings blessings and evil ultimately brings cursings, there are short-term exceptions. Sometimes in this life the wicked prosper and the righteous suffer (Ps. 73; Job 1—2). The full understanding of the death of good King Josiah at the hands of Pharaoh

Neco is hidden in the mysteries of God's providence. The later historian attributed his death to his refusal to listen to the word of God that came to him through the warning of Pharaoh Neco not to interfere in his plan to fight the Assyrians at Carchemish (2 Chron. 35:22).

The Reign of Jehoahaz (23:31-35)

Jehoahaz reflected the true nature of his people in reverting to the evil practices of Manasseh and Amon and other wicked kings of Judah. The defeat of Josiah by Pharaoh Neco at Megiddo gave the Egyptians supreme power over Judah. Accordingly, Pharaoh Neco deported to Egypt King Jehoahaz after a three-month reign and replaced him with Jehoahaz's brother Eliakim whom Neco renamed Jehoiakim.

The Reign of Jehoiakim: The Beginning of Captivity (23:36 to 24:7)

Jeremiah the prophet, who spoke several of his prophecies during the reign of Jehoiakim, confirmed the evil nature of Jehoiakim. See Jeremiah 22:13-19; 25; 26; 35; 45. The word of the Lord to Jeremiah indicates that God would have been willing to save Judah had the people repented (Jer. 36:2-3). But the cutting up and burning of the word of God by Jehoiakim confirmed once again the depth of their apostasy (Jer. 36:22-26).

The Babylonians conquered Ninevah, the capital of Assyria, in 612 BC, and the Babylonian Empire led by Nabopolassar and his son Nebuchadnezzar spread its influence across the Middle East as far south as Egypt (24:7). Jehoiakim submitted himself at first to Nebuchadnezzar, but then rebelled against him (24:1). The marauders whom God sent upon Judah ushered in the beginning of the end according to prophecy (24:2-4). Among these marauders were "the Chaldeans," that is, the Babylonians, led by Nebuchadnezzar. He conquered the city of Jerusalem in the third/fourth year of Jehoiakim, which was also the first year of his reign as king of Babylon (Dan. 1:1; Jer. 25:1). In the first stage of captivity, Nebuchadnezzar took to Babylon some of the vessels of the house of the Lord and Daniel and some choice Hebrew youth (Dan. 1:1-4).

The Reign of Jehoiachin: The Second Stage of Captivity (24:8-17)

In the eighth year of his reign (597 BC), Nebuchadnezzar accepted the surrender of Jehoiachin and his royal household, probably with the understanding that the city would be spared. At that time, Nebuchadnezzar deported to Babylon the king, the men of valor, and all the notables of Jerusalem, leaving only the poorest of the land (24:12-16). Nebuchadnezzar made Mattaniah, the uncle of King Jehoiachin, king in his stead, and changed his name to Zedekiah (24:17).

The Reign of Zedekiah: The Final Stage of Exile (24:18 to 25:21)

After the normal introduction to the wicked reign of Zedekiah's (24:18-24a), this passage describes Zedekiah's rebellion against the king of Babylon and his horrible fate (24:20b to 25:7), the burning of the house of God and of the city of Jerusalem and the Exile of the people to Babylon (25:8-12), the plundering of the house of God (25:13-17), execution of Judah's leaders (25:18-21a), and a summary statement of the Exile of Judah (25:21b).

"The anger of the Lord" (24:20) that brought about the desolation was evoked by the terrible sin of the people. The later historian described the moral pollution of the king, the priests, and the people as well as their persistent refusal to humble themselves before God until there was no remedy for their sins except destruction (2 Chron. 36:11-16).

Zedekiah's rebellion against Nebuchadnezzar was probably encouraged by the military resurgence of Egypt. Moreover, the movement of the Egyptian forces doubtless helped Jerusalem to withstand the Babylonian siege for nineteen months (Jer. 37:5-12). But the city finally fell on the seventh day of July/August, 586 BC, which was in the eleventh year of the reign of Zedekiah and the eighteenth/nineteenth year of King Nebuchadnezzar (25:2, 8; Jer. 52:29).

Two Appendixes: Aftermath of Jerusalem's Fall (25:22-30)

The first appendix reports on Gedaliah's governorship of Judah (vv. 22-26). The Babylonians left in Judah only the poorest of the people to cultivate the land (v. 12). Gedaliah, whom Nebuchadnezzar set over the remaining people, was himself from a prominent family. His father Ahikim was influential enough in the reign of Jehoiakim to save Jeremiah the prophet from death (Jer. 26:24). His grandfather Shaphan was secretary to King Josiah and figured prominently in his efforts to turn the people back to God (2 Kings 22:3 ff.). Gedaliah himself returned brokenhearted Jeremiah back to his home after the fall of Jerusalem (Jer. 39:14). The men who rallied around Gedaliah at Mizpah were soldiers who were scattered before, during, and after the siege of Jerusalem (vv. 22-24). See Jeremiah 41-43 for details concerning the assassination of Gedaliah and the migration against the will of God of Jeremiah and the remaining Judahites (v. 26).

The second appendix reports on Evil-merodach's gracious care of Jehoiachin (vv. 27-30). Seemingly, this record was included as a prelude of the good that was yet to come in God's gracious providence for his people.

2 CHRONICLES

Introduction

Second Chronicles is the second of a four-book series that includes 1 and 2 Chronicles, Ezra, and Nehemiah. These books provide a scribal (priestly) history of Israel from the time of Saul's death to the rebuilding of the house of God and the walls of Jerusalem.

The special focus of these books is on the fortunes of the house of God in Jerusalem upon which God has set his name forever. David prepared to build the house of God, Solomon did the building, and Zerubbabel rebuilt the house of God. The kings of Judah throughout were judged by whether or not they were faithful to the house of God.

The Hebrew name for Chronicles means "the acts or deeds of the day or times." Second Chronicles itself encompasses the reign of Solomon (1:1 to 9:31), the reigns of the kings of Judah from the division of the kingdom in the days of Rehoboam the son of Solomon to the Babylonian captivity (10:1 to 36:21), and finally as an appendix the divinely-inspired decree of Cyrus the king of the Medo-Persian Empire by which the Jews were encouraged to return to Jerusalem to rebuild the house of God (36:22-23). The kings of the Northern Kingdom are mentioned only as they relate to the kings of Judah. They are not included for themselves, inasmuch as they stood in rebellion to the house of David that continued to be represented in the kings of Judah.

Ancient tradition names Ezra the scribe as the author of 2 Chronicles. Ezra is distinguished as the scribe who prepared his heart to understand, to keep, and to teach in Israel the law of the Lord (Ezra 7:10). The position of 2 Chronicles in the *Hagiographa*, the last division of the Hebrew canon, indicates that the author was not a prophet. Moreover, the emphasis upon the priests and other Levites suggests as author someone out of their own ranks.

The author of 2 Chronicles, whom we shall call the Chronicler, focused on the blessings that attended the kings and the people who were faithful to the house of God and on the curses that came on the kings and the people who were faithless to the house of God. By this historical demonstration of the value of loyalty to God and to his house, the

102

Chronicler sought to encourage the people of his day and of every generation to be faithful to God and his house and to worship therein according to the law of Moses.

The Chronicler had other purposes in writing. One was to supplement the material concerning the kings of Judah found in Kings. That purpose is implied in the Septuagint name for Chronicles, meaning "things left over." Another purpose was to magnify the role of the priests and other Levites who were ordained of God to care for God's house and to teach his Word. A third was to clarify the correct interpretation of certain events mentioned in Kings. See commentary on 2 Chronicles 10:1 to 12:16 for a case in point. The classic example of the Chronicler's clarifying the prophetic interpretation is his noting that the census for which God punished David was allowed by God, but actually inspired by Satan (2 Sam. 24:1; 1 Chron. 21:1).

The Reign of Solomon
1:1 to 9:31

Solomon's Early Reign: His Wisdom and Prosperity (1:1-17)

The connective "and" (v. 1) indicates that 2 Chronicles continues the scribal history of Israel recorded in 1 Chronicles, which concluded with a summary of the reign of David (1 Chron. 29:26-30). This section, which focuses on Solomon's God-given wisdom and prosperity, serves as an introduction to the reign of Solomon. The Chronicler's purpose to magnify Solomon's greatest work, namely, that of building and dedicating the house of God, is seen in his passing over many of the events in Solomon's life recorded in the Book of 1 Kings and in his treating in summary fashion those matters included (1 Kings 1:1 to 11:43).

Second Chronicles picks up with Solomon's establishment of himself as king and the blessings of God by which he became great (v. 1). Although Adonijah's plot to be king is not described (1 Kings 1:5-10), these opening words allude to the internal struggles for the throne by which Solomon was established as David's successor according to the providence of God.

Attention is next given to Solomon's assembly of the officials and the people for the religious service at Gibeon by which Solomon invoked

God's blessings upon his reign (vv. 2-6). The Chronicler told of the presence of the Mosaic tent of meeting and bronze altar at Gibeon in order to explain why Solomon would have chosen Gibeon as the high place for the sacrifices to God. Note, however, the commentary on 1 Kings 3:1-3 to see that his offering sacrifices to God at any high place was sin.

The Chronicler next described God's appearance to Solomon at Gibeon and his promise to him of wisdom and wealth in response to Solomon's prayer (vv. 7-13). The appearance of God at night points to a dream vision as is noted specifically in 1 Kings 3:5. The deliberate omission in the vision of reference to God's conditional promise of long life to Solomon for his obedience to God (1 Kings 3:14) indicates that the Chronicler was aware of Solomon's moral failures and intentionally projected an ideal picture of Solomon. It is almost as if Solomon's building the Temple caused the inspired interpreter to overlook the bad in Solomon's life.

This section closes with a description of Solomon's wealth and honor to show that God fulfilled his promise to Solomon (vv. 14-17). The Chronicler added "gold" (v. 15) to the nearly word-for-word description of Solomon's wealth and honor found in 1 Kings 10:26-29. In noting that God gave to Solomon the wealth and honor for which he did not ask, the Chronicler implied that God also gave him the wisdom and knowledge to rule well for which he did ask. Note, however, the commentary on 1 Kings 3:4-15 to see that Solomon failed to ask God for the higher wisdom that would have led to his wholehearted obedience to God and to perfect fulfillment of God's purposes for him.

Solomon's Building and Dedication of the House of God (2:1 to 7:22)

His Preparation (2:1-18)

After noting Solomon's purpose to build the Temple for the name of God and a royal palace for himself (v. 1), the Chronicler focused on the preparation Solomon made to build the house of God (vv. 2-18). Solomon's work could be labeled "final preparation," since David himself made extensive provisions prior to his death for constructing the house of God. Indeed, David had set aliens to work preparing dressed stones for the building of the house of God (1 Chron. 22:2), had provided great stores of nails, clamps, bronze, and timber (1 Chron. 22:3-5), had placed in Solomon's hands the complete God-given plan for the Temple

(1 Chron. 28:11-19), and had himself contributed and encouraged others to contribute great quantities of gold and silver, iron and bronze, and jewels and marble (1 Chron. 29:1-9).

In spelling out Solomon's preparation for building the house of God, the Chronicler noted: (1) his assignment of slave labor for building (v. 2); (2) his arrangement with "Huram"—an alternate spelling of "Hiram"—king of Tyre for a skilled man and timber for the construction (vv. 3-16); and (3) his census of aliens by which slave labor was obtained (vv. 17-18). Solomon, in requesting Hiram's help, boldly bore witness to the Lord God of Israel as "greater than all gods" (v. 5). Hiram's response to Solomon's request was twofold. First, he praised "the Lord God of Israel" (v. 12) for giving David such a wise son to build the Temple and royal palace (vv. 11-12). His use of God's personal name ("Lord" is Yahweh), plus his reference to him as the creator of heaven and earth, perhaps indicates that Hiram himself was a believer in the Lord God of Israel. Second, Hiram sent the needed skilled workers and arranged for the necessary timber (vv. 13-16). The Chronicler indicated that "Huram-abi," which means "Hiram is my father," or "Hiram" for short, was skilled in working with gold, silver, iron, stone, wood, and fabrics, as well as bronze (v. 14; 1 Kings 7:13).

Construction of the Temple (3:1-17)

The Chronicler first noted that Solomon built the Temple on Mount Moriah at the threshing floor of Ornan the Jebusite, which was the divinely-appointed site specified by David (v. 1). "Mount Moriah" (v. 1) identified the site as the place where Abraham had prepared Isaac for sacrifice to the Lord in obedience to God's command, but where God stayed his hand from taking the child's life and provided instead the ram for sacrifice (Gen. 22:1-14). Then the Chronicler dated the beginning of the building of the Temple in the second month of the fourth year of Solomon's reign (v. 2). Although Solomon was in total sympathy with his God-given responsibility to build the Temple, the delay until the fourth year of his reign was necessitated by the required preparation outlined in 2:1-18. Finally, the Chronicler in this section gave details concerning the measurements and construction of the vestibule and nave (vv. 3-7), of the holy of holies and its furnishings (vv. 8-14), and of the pillars in front of the Temple. For dimensions of the Temple and its various segments figured on an eighteen-inch cubit, see commentary on 1 Kings 5:1 to 6:38. However, note that the "cubits of the old standard" (v. 3) may have been twenty-one inches instead of eighteen. If that were the case, the dimensions of the Temple noted in the commentary on Kings would have to be altered by adding three inches for every cubit. That would make, for example, the overall length of the house of God including the vestibule one hundred and forty feet instead of one hundred and five feet. Even then the house of God was quite small by modern standards. However, what it lacked in size was more than compensated by quality. Six hundred talents of gold, for example, were used to overlay the walls in the holy of holies (v. 8). Figuring a talent at seventy-five pounds, this amount of gold was worth hundreds of millions of dollars in today's terms. Even some of the nails used to attach the gold to the walls of the holy of holies were "fifty shekels of gold," that is, twenty ounces of gold. "A hundred and twenty cubits" (v. 4) for the height of the vestibule is probably a scribal error. The veil, not mentioned in 1 Kings, was made exactly as the veil in the tabernacle, that is, with the same materials and colors and interwoven cherubims (Ex. 26:31). See commentary on 1 Kings 7:13-51 for the significance of the two pillars, "Jachin" and "Boaz."

The Furnishings of the Temple (4:1 to 5:1)

The Chronicler described the furnishings of the house of God, which were made by Solomon through Hiram the artisan of Tyre and the skilled workers whom he directed. Included are the bronze altar (v. 1), the molten sea (vv. 2-6), the ten lampstands (v. 7), the ten tables (v. 8a), the hundred basins of gold (v. 8b), the courts (v. 9), the placement of the molten sea (v. 10), and additional works of Hiram, such as pots and shovels (vv. 11-18). The altar of bronze, the making of which is not described in 1 Kings, was a rectangle thirty feet long, thirty feet wide, and fifteen feet high. It was modeled after the altar of Bezalel in the tabernacle, although much larger (Ex. 27:1-8). It apparently was approached by steps and used for all sacrifices. Its position at the threshold of the house of God clearly taught that man could not approach God except through blood sacrifices.

The molten sea, whose capacity is said by the Chronicler to be three thousand baths (one bath equals a little more than six gallons) instead of the two thousand baths noted in 1 Kings 7:26, was used for the priests to wash themselves. It stood upon twelve oxen, which symbolized the twelve tribes of Israel as God's servants. The arrangement in four groups of three facing each direction of the compass probably reminded them of how they were gathered as a nation in tribes about the tabernacle in the wilderness journey to the Promised Land (Num. 2:1-34). The ten lavers or basins, which stood upon the brazen stands on either side of the molten sea (1 Kings 7:30), were for washing the burnt offering. The ten tables may have been used for the ten lampstands but more likely for shewbread. The hundred basins of gold were used for dashing the sacrificial blood against the altar. The Chronicler concluded this section with a summary statement concerning the completion of all of the furnishings of the Temple and a notation of Solomon's storing in the Temple treasury the gifts of David for the house of God (4:19 to 5:1; 1 Chron. 18:11; 26:26).

Transfer of the Ark (5:2-10)

Upon completion of the Temple, Solomon assembled the leaders of Israel for the priests and Levites to transfer the ark and the rest of the tabernacle from Zion to the Temple (vv. 2-4). God had consecrated the Levites for the most holy task of carrying the ark of the Lord and the rest of the tabernacle (Deut. 10:8; 31:25; Num. 1:40-51; 3:31). David learned from bitter experience not to violate this sacred trust that belonged alone to the Levites (2 Sam. 6:6-11; 1 Chron. 15:1-2; 16:1). From the Levites through the line of Aaron also came the priests. As such, the sons of Aaron were priests as well as Levites and could discharge any service of the Levites. Accordingly, the Levites who took up the ark of God were also priests (vv. 4,7; 1 Kings 8:3). These priests were joined with other Levites in bringing up the tabernacle and all of its furnishings into the house of God (v. 5). However, the priests themselves brought the ark into its permanent resting place in the holy of holies under the cherubim whose wings formed a canopy over it and the poles by which it was carried (vv. 7-8). "They are there to this day" (v. 9), which refers to the poles by which the ark was carried and which extended beyond the veil that hid the ark, illustrates the Chronicler's faithfulness to his sources. Although the Temple had been destroyed and the ark lost by the time he wrote, he carefully preserved even the words of his source. The ark contained only the two tables of stone on which God wrote the Ten Commandments (v. 10). The later notation that the ark also "contained a golden urn holding the manna, and Aaron's rod that budded" (Heb. 9:4) is to be interpreted as meaning that the manna and rod were before the ark rather than in it (Ex. 16:32-33). The manna and the rod reminded the Israelites of the wondrous works by which the Lord God sought to teach them to trust and obey him. For the significance of the two tables of stone, see commentary in 1 Kings 8:1 to 9:9.

The Appearance of the Glory of the Lord Filling the Temple (5:11-14)

When the priests and Levites came out of the Temple and the Levitical choir began to sing (vv. 11-13a). God consecrated the house of the Lord by filling it with his glory (vv. 13b-14). "The Glory of the Lord" (v.14) is the designation for the fiery presence of God by which he revealed himself. God's glory is basically whatever makes him majestic in the eyes of people. Since God's character gives him majesty, God's revelation of his character is called his glory. Moreover, since the fiery presence by which God revealed his holiness made such a tremendous impact upon people, God's fiery presence was also called "the glory of the Lord."

"A cloud" (v. 13) is "the cloud" (v. 14) by which God shrouded his glorious presence. This fiery cloud was first seen by Moses and the Israelites as God thereby led them victoriously out of the land of Egypt (Ex. 13:21-22). The immediate purpose of the fiery cloud was so that the Israelites could travel "by day and night" (Ex. 13:21). The second purpose was to make the Israelites aware that the Lord God himself was leading them and to inspire them to believe in him (Ex. 14:31). The fiery cloud was next seen by the Israelites in the Wilderness of Sin as God displayed his anger at the murmuring of the people (Ex. 16:10-12). The cloud, which was described as thick or dark, provided a covering for the glory of the Lord on Mount Sinai (Ex. 19:9,16). Moses explained that God had so revealed himself to them to test them and to fill them with dread of offending him (Ex. 20:20). Moses also saw the Lord in this cloud on Mount Sinai in the Lord's revealing to Moses his name, that is, his character (Ex. 34:5-7). Then, when Moses and the people raised the tabernacle, which had been built according to God's plan for approaching him, the glory of God shrouded by this cloud covered and indwelt the tabernacle. That great fact symbolized that God was among his people. Thereafter God continued in their midst in this fiery cloud to instruct, protect, guide, and sanctify them (Ex. 40:36-38).

The Levitical choir had been organized by David. Actually, David organized the Levites, which included the priests, into five classes: (1) the sons of Aaron who served as priests; (2) those who assisted the priestly Levites in the prescribed work of the sanctuary; (3) those who served as scribes and judges to preserve and teach the word of God and to govern the people thereby; (4) those who kept the gates of the house of the Lord to assure that the law of Moses was kept; and (5) those who offered praise to God with musical instruments and song. See 1 Chronicles 23:2-6. Each of these classes, with the possible exception of the scribes and the judges, were further divided into twenty-four groups to serve in rotation, so that their ministries at the Temple were always provided (1 Chron. 24:1 to 26:33). However, the bringing of the ark into the house of God was such a great event that the Levites were on hand to serve in the respective ministries without regard to their divisions (vv. 11-12).

Further Dedication and Consecration of the Temple (6:1 to 7:10)

The Chronicler noted in this section: (1) Solomon's response to the glory of God filling the Temple (6:1-12); (2) Solomon's dedicatory address (6:3-11); (3) Solomon's dedicatory prayer (6:12-42); (4) the Lord's approving response by which he further consecrated the house of God (7:1-3); (5) additional sacrifices and praise by Solomon and the people (7:4-6); (6) the dedication of the middle of the court (7:7); and (7) the dedicatory feast (7:8-10).

The heart of Solomon's dedicatory address is praise of God for fulfilling his promise to David in establishing him as king in his father's stead and in consecrating with his glorious presence the house that Solomon had built for the name of the Lord. The notation that God made the covenant with "the people of Israel" (v. 11) as well as with the Hebrew fathers (1 Kings 8:21) emphasizes that God's intent for his covenant people is a united Israel under the throne of David.

Solomon's dedicatory prayer included: (1) Solomon's position in prayer (6:12-13); (2) his praise of God for God's greatness in keeping his covenant with his obedient servants in general and with David in particular (6:14-15); (3) his petition that God continue to keep his covenant with David through David's sons (6:16-17); (4) his petition that God would make the house of the Lord the place where he and the people could meet with God, have their prayers answered, and find forgiveness (6:18-21); (5) his prayer that God would hear and answer seven particular petitions (6:22-40); and (6) the conclusion of his prayer (6:41-42). The first of the seven specific prayers is the oath of innocency by which God was asked to confirm by action at his house the avowed innocency of the just, but to condemn those who claimed innocency, but were guilty of the trespass (6:22-23). The second is the prayer for forgiveness and restoration to overcome sin-produced national defeat and exile (6:24-25). The third is the prayer for forgiveness and rain to overcome sin-produced drought (6:26-27). The fourth is the prayer for forgiveness and healing of the land to overcome sin-produced famine, pestilence or whatever affliction (6:28-31). The fifth is to hear the foreigner's prayer for forgiveness and knowledge of God (6:32-33). The sixth is the prayer of soldiers for military victory in divinely directed battles (6:34-35). The seventh is the prayer of repentant people in sin-produced exile for compassion at the hands of their captors (6:36-39). Solomon's conclusion to his prayer was actually a twofold petition. First, he besought God to take up his abode among them in the Temple so that in partaking of his Glory the priests would be clothed with salvation and the saints would rejoice in his goodness (6:41). Note that "thy resting place" implied God's permanent dwelling in his house among his people. Second, he besought God not to turn away his face from "thy anointed one" (the king), but to continue for the sake of David to maintain covenant with the sons of David by means of his steadfast and righteous love (6:42).

God registered his approval of Solomon's dedication of the Temple in two ways. First, he sent fire from heaven to ignite the altar and to consume the sacrifices that had been offered (7:1a; 5:6). Fire had come from God to devour David's sacrifices to God on the threshing floor of Ornan, to stay the plague, as well as at other times (1 Chron. 21:26; Judg. 6:21). However, the fire that came from God at the dedication of the Temple seems to have its parallel in the fire that came from God to ignite the altar fire of the tabernacle that the priests were to keep burning (Lev. 9:23-24; 6:12-13). Accordingly, God himself consecrated the Temple as the one and only place for sacrifice by igniting the altar fire. Second, God filled the Temple once again with his glorious presence (7:1b). Apparently, simultaneously with his sending the fire from heaven to devour the sacrifices, God caused the fire of his presence shrouded by cloud to fill the interior of the house of God. The priests were prohibited from performing their tasks both by their awe at the fire that had come from heaven and the devouring presence of God seen in the Temple (7:2). The supernatural nature of the fire of God's presence is seen in its not burning up the house of God. This double manifestation of God's presence with them by which he had consecrated the Temple for worship brought reverence, worship, and thanksgiving among the people (7:3).

"David offered praises by their ministry" (v. 6) provides a beautiful insight into what happens in the case of those who make possible or assist in a particular ministry. David had organized and equipped with musical instruments the Levitical choir. Accordingly, their ministry at the house of God was also his ministry in that he served through them.

The Lord's Appearance to Solomon (7:11-22)

As noted in the commentary on 1 Kings 9:1-9, God appeared this second time to Solomon some time after the twenty years required to build the house of God and Solomon's palace. As also noted, this appearance of God, in which God issued Solomon conditional promises and warnings, was occasioned most likely by Solomon's slipping deeper and deeper into sin. God initially reminded Solomon that he had heard Solomon's prayer and had chosen "as a house of sacrifice" the Temple Solomon had built and consecrated to God nine years earlier (v. 12). "A house of sacrifice" should be rendered "for house of sacrifice," so as to make clear its being the one and only place of sacrifice.

Then God made four pledges to Solomon. First, God promised to forgive his people and to heal their land upon their repenting and praying (vv. 13-14). "Who are called by my name" identifies "my people" literally as "those upon whom my name has been called." Israel had entered into a covenant with God based on their trust and obedience, by which they were his very own treasured people, missionary people, and holy people (Ex. 19:4-6). God had marked Israel as his very own by putting his name upon them. If they dishonored his name by their rebellious living, he would bring upon them chastisement by which they would be purified. Drought, devouring locust, and pestilence are three expressions of the chastening curse that God had vowed to bring upon the people in the Promised Land if they failed to obey him (Deut. 28:15-68). This chastening curse also included invasion of and even expulsion from the land and exile among foreign nations if they persisted in their wickedness (Deut. 28:49-68). However, God would not give them up (Deut. 30:1-10) nor fail to fulfill his vow to have a son of David on the throne in Jerusalem where he had set his name (2 Sam. 7:12-16; Ps. 89:34-36).

"Humble themselves" indicates that God's covenant people, which in its larger sense includes all believers, would need to take hold of their own hearts and submit themselves to God. "Pray" carries the idea of prostrating oneself before God to ask him to stay the curses and to restore his blessings upon the Land. The basic ideas in "pray" are to judge and to intercede. Accordingly, God's people judge themselves to be guilty of their sin that caused the curses and intercede with God to forgive them and to restore his blessings. "Seek" carries the basic idea of "searching until one finds." Accordingly, "seek my face" means to search after God in humility and prayer until they had found again his favor. "And turn from their wicked ways" means that their humbling themselves before God in prayer seeking to restore themselves again to God's favor must be accompanied by genuine repentance. "Turn," which is the basic word for repentance, carries both the idea of turning oneself and then of returning. Accordingly, genuine repentance would involve turning from their wicked ways *and* returning to the true worship of God as prescribed in the law of Moses. "Their wicked ways" certainly describes any and all sin. Reference, however, is specifically to those attitudes and practices that were especially displeasing to the Lord. "Wicked" is "the evil" and denotes the heinous sins of the Canaanites that defiled the land of Canaan and that led to their expulsion from the land. Elsewhere, these sinful attitudes and practices are called "evil in the sight of the Lord" (Judg. 2:11; 4:1; and so forth). In Leviticus 18:1-30, these sins, which are called "abominable customs" (v. 30), are described somewhat. Included are: sexual sin with so-called "blood relatives" and other kin (vv. 6-18), sexual relations with a woman during her menstrual period (v. 19), sexual relations with a neighbor's wife (v. 20), child sacrifice (v. 21), sexual relations with the same gender (v. 22), and sexual relations with animals (v. 23). "Hear . . . forgive . . . and heal" denote God's promise not merely to stay the curses, but to forgive their sin and make the Land once again delightsome when they met his conditions of humbling themselves, seeking his face, praying, and turning from their wicked ways.

Second, God pledged to be attentive to the prayers made in the house of the Lord (vv. 15-16). This included God's promise to hear and act on the specific requests Solomon had made in his dedicatory prayer (6:22-42).

Third, God pledged to establish forever on the throne of David the seed of Solomon if Solomon would walk obediently in the ways of the Lord as David his father did (vv. 17-18). A distinction is to be made between the throne of Solomon and the seed of Solomon. Solomon's throne as a continuation of David's dynasty was eternally established by the promise of God to David (2 Sam. 7:12-13; Ps. 89:34-36). However, whether the eternal ruling line would be of David through Solomon was conditioned on Solomon's obedience. The sin of Solomon, which reached its climax in Ahaz's refusal to receive the sign of God (Isa. 7:10-14) and in the wicked reign of Manasseh that brought the expulsion of the people from the Promised Land (2 Kings 21:10-15), caused Solomon's seed to be cut off.

Fourth, God pledged to make judgment proverbs out of the people of Israel and the house of God if Solomon and the people turned from God's way to serve other gods (vv. 19-22). Their sin would result in God's driving them out of the Land and in his desolating the house of God. These judgments would be intended to bring the Israelites back to God, but would not result in the forfeiture of God's covenant with the people of Israel and/or with David. The Christ—the true son of David —will reign over all of the people of God.

Solomon's Other Achievements (8:1-18)

The building of the house of God was Solomon's greatest achievement. Accordingly, all of Solomon's other achievements, which were quite extensive, were given only summary treatment by the Chronicler. The Chronicler briefly noted: (1) Solomon's building, rebuilding, and fortifying cities (vv. 1-6); (2) his forcing aliens into labor battalions (vv. 7-10); (3) his moving his wife—Pharaoh's daughter—to the house in the royal palace he had prepared for her (v. 11); (4) his provision for and regulation of public worship according to the law of Moses and the ordinance of David (vv. 12-16); and (5) his profitable maritime ventures (vv. 17-18).

Not only had Solomon given Hiram twenty cities (1 Kings 9:11-14), but Hiram gave certain cities to Solomon (v. 2). Some interpreters take these to be the same cities. They believe that Hiram returned to Solomon as worthless the cities Solomon had given to him in exchange for gold and that Solomon thereafter restored them. Archaeological discoveries at Gezer, Megiddo, Hazor, Ezion-geber, and other places bear witness to Solomon's building activities. Remains at Meggido, for example, especially those of Solomon's stables that provided for as many as four hundred and fifty horses and one hundred and fifty chariots, show that Solomon transformed that urban center into a chariot city to give him an iron grip on the strategic passes and trade routes related to the Plains of Jezreel. His large smelting furnaces for copper and iron uncovered at Ezion-geber are another example of Solomon's vast enterprises. Solomon's enslavement of Canaanite aliens for forced labor (vv. 7-10) perhaps goes back to Joshua's curse upon the Gibeonites for their deception of the Israelites. They were allowed to remain in the Land as perpetual servants rather than being exterminated because of the sanctity of the oath of the princes of Israel (Josh. 9:15,22-23). For the number of forced laborers and the relationship of the Israelites to them, see commentary on 1 Kings 5:13-18. The house for Pharaoh's daughter to which Solomon moved her from the city of David apparently was part of the palace complex (1 Kings 3:1; 7:8); however, it was far enough removed so as not to defile God's house (2 Chron. 8:11).

"Solomon offered up burnt offerings" (v. 12) means that Solomon directed the worship activities so that public worship was carried out according to the commandments of Moses, not that he himself usurped the role of priests in performing their functions. "According to the ordinance of David" (v. 14) indicates that Solomon took the action prescribed by David to ensure that there would always be Levites at the house of God (1) to perform the priestly services, (2) to help the Levitical priests in their functions, (3) to guard the several gates of the Temple area, and (4) to offer praises to God with instruments and song. For David's ordinance of the Levites, see 1 Chronicles 23—26 and commentary on 2 Chronicles 5:11-13.

"Eloth" (modern Elath) was on the northern shore of the Gulf of Aqaba and was early spoken of in connection with Ezion-geber. Ezion-geber was perhaps slightly to the west of Eloth. However, many interpreters take Eloth to be in opposition to Ezion-geber as its later name. Certainly after Eloth was rebuilt by Uzziah (Azariah) (2 Kings 14:22; 2 Chron. 26:2), it seems to encompass Ezion-geber. Eloth was a strategic city because the ancient caravan route between Southern Arabia, Egypt, and Phoenicia ran by its gates. How Hiram got the ships to Solomon is not known. There was no Suez Canal then, so that the only waterway would have been to sail around the southern tip of Africa. Most likely, Hiram's sailors and other workers carried the ships in sections across the overland route and assembled them at Eloth.

Solomon's Wisdom and Wealth and Fame (9:1-28)

The visit of the queen of Sheba illustrates Solomon's international fame (vv. 1-12). Sheba, which is connected by Josephus with Egypt and Ethiopia, was most likely located at the southern tip of Arabia where the Red Sea joins the Arabian Sea. Jesus himself spoke of the queen of Sheba as "the queen of the South" (Matt. 12:42). The Sabeans, as the inhabitants of Sheba were called, were great traders who merchandised their own products as well as those of Ethiopia and India. They were noted for their gold, incense, and precious stones (v. 1; Ezek. 27:23). The queen perhaps first heard of Solomon's wisdom and wealth from her own traders and also those from the ships of Solomon that sailed the Red Sea to purchase the gold of Ophir (v. 10). (Ophir was perhaps also located in southern Arabia adjoining Sheba to the west by northwest.)

Jesus implied that the queen's purpose "to test" (v. 1) Solomon was related to her higher desire to know the wisdom and salvation of God found in Solomon, inasmuch as she shall condemn in the judgment those who reject the wisdom and salvation of God found in Jesus (Matt. 12:42). "The hard questions" (v. 1) with which she proved him were literally riddles or obscure sayings that hinted at deeper truths. "No more spirit in her" (v. 4) means that the queen was totally deflated and awe-struck by the glory of Solomon reflected in his wisdom, his buildings, his royal provisions, and his worship.

As befitting the queen of a rich country, she brought a large number of expensive gifts to Solomon (vv. 1,9). Indeed, the one hundred and twenty talents of gold that she gave him would be worth millions of dollars in today's terms. The spices she gave to him in "very great quantity," which could not be found at that time at any other place, included frankincense and myrrh, both of which were later immortalized by the gifts of the Magi to the Christ child (Matt. 2:11). Solomon in turn gave gifts to the queen (v. 12). "Whatever she asked besides what she had brought to the king" indicates that his gifts to her extended far beyond those required by international protocol and included whatever her heart desired. Her tribute to Solomon also included praise to the Lord God of Israel for giving to Solomon such a glorious kingdom (vv. 5-8, esp. v. 8).

Next the Chronicler illustrated the wealth and wisdom of Solomon (vv. 13-28). Described first is his great store of gold and implements of gold (vv. 13-21). His yearly income of six hundred and sixty-six talents of gold compare to a yearly income today of hundreds of millions of dollars. He received in addition great amounts of gold from tolls and tribute paid by merchants and vassal kings. Each shekel weighs about .025 pounds, with six hundred shekels totaling about fifteen pounds. Accordingly, each of the two hundred large gold shields with which he decorated the House of the Forest of Lebanon was immensely valuable. His great throne, made of ivory overlaid with gold, with six steps and a footstool of gold, was more splendid than the throne of any other kingdom.

Described second is Solomon's wisdom (vv. 22-28). In wisdom as well as in riches, Solomon was greater than all the kings of the earth (v. 22). His wisdom in fact increased his riches, for kings of all the earth brought him lavish gifts of great worth in their coming to him for the wisdom God had put in his heart (vv. 23-24). Solomon's empire over which he ruled in glory extended all the way to the Euphrates River in the north to the Egyptian border in the south, with a small section next to the Mediterranean Sea occupied by the Philistines (v. 26). Thus, God in fulfillment of his promise gave to Solomon riches and honor as well as wisdom.

Conclusion of Solomon's Reign (9:29-31)

This brief concluding notation describes other sources concerning Solomon's reign (v. 29), the length of Solomon's reign (v. 30), and finally his death, burial, and successor. Nathan, Ahijah the Shilonite, and Iddo the seer are here stated to have provided specific written records which could be investigated for additional information concerning the reign of Solomon. Nathan was the distinguished prophet during the days of David and Solomon (1 Kings 1:8,10-11, and so forth). Ahijah was the prophet of Shiloh in the latter reign of Solomon who most likely predicted to Solomon the division of the kingdom (1 Kings 10:11-13), who did predict dramatically to Jeroboam that he would rule over ten tribes of the divided kingdom (1 Kings 11:29-39), and who did predict the tearing of the kingdom from the house of Jeroboam (1 Kings 14:1-18). Nothing is known concerning Iddo the seer except that he wrote prophetic visions. His visions concerning Jeroboam the son of Nebat included events of Solomon's reign. Also he wrote prophetic visions concerning the reigns of Rehoboam and Ahijah (2 Chron. 12:15; 13:22). "History," which literally means "words" or "discourse," probably describes Nathan's work as broader in scope than that of Ahijah or of Iddo. "Prophecy" and "vision" perhaps indicate that Ahijah's and Iddo's writings were restricted to their own prophecies and visions. "Prophet" and "prophecy" are basic words for the man of God and his message. Built on the root *to speak*, these words magnify the prophet's role of spokesman for God. "Seer" and "visions" are additional words for the prophet and his message. Both of these words are built on the root *to see* and *to perceive*. As such, these words focus on the ability of the man of God to perceive the significance of a certain event or prophetic vision. "Visions" probably denotes the major way that God communicated with Iddo.

The Chronicler closes his discussion of the reign of Solomon without any reference to Solomon's apostasy or to the division of the kingdom that would come because of Solomon's apostasy. Characteristic of his desire to picture Solomon in an ideal light, the Chronicler wanted the last thoughts of Solomon to be good.

The Reigns of the Kings of Judah from the Division of the Kingdom to the Babylonian Captivity
10:1 to 36:23

The united Hebrew kingdom was divided at the beginning of the reign of Rehoboam, the son and successor of Solomon to the Davidic throne, into the Northern and Southern Kingdoms. Judah and Benjamin, which composed the Southern Kingdom, stayed true to the dynasty of David. But the remaining ten tribes rebelled against the house of David and started their own kingdom under Jeroboam the son of Nebat. True Israel was to be found in those people over whom the house of David ruled from his throne in Jerusalem. As such, the Southern Kingdom, which came to be known as Judah, was alone considered by the Chronicler to be true Israel. Therefore, the Chronicler concentrated on the reigns of the kings of Judah to the exclusion of Northern Israel. Indeed, he considered the Northern Kingdom only at those times when its history vitally touched the affairs of Judah. The record of the reigns of the kings of Judah found in 2 Chronicles 10:1 to 36:21 follows closely those found for the rulers of Judah in the Books of Kings. However, characteristically, the Chronicler treats the reigns of the kings of Judah in more detail than the author of the Books of Kings.

The Reign of Rehoboam (10:1 to 12:16)

The Rebellion of Israel (10:1-19)

Rehoboam was readily accepted as king over Judah. However, when he journeyed to Shechem to receive the crown of the ten tribes of Israel (v. 1), he met with great difficulty. See commentary on 1 Kings 12:1-24 for the tenuous nature of the union of the Southern and Northern Kingdoms. The elders of the ten tribes of Israel, led by Jeroboam the son of Nebat, demanded that Rehoboam lift the grievous burdens imposed on them by Solomon for his extravagant building programs (vv. 2-4). Rehoboam sent these elders away for a three-day period in which he would decide what to do about their request (v. 5). During this time, Rehoboam sought counsel concerning the action he should take (vv. 5-11). The older men who had given counsel to Solomon advised him to grant their request (vv. 5-8). However, he accepted the counsel of the younger men who had grown up with him to increase their burdens. "If you will be kind to this people and please them" illustrates how the Chronicler changed the wording to avoid misinterpretation of the statement, "If you will be a servant to this people today and serve them" (1 Kings 12:7). As found in 1 Kings, the elders' suggestion could be interpreted to mean that Rehoboam should vow to do anything the people wanted to obtain acceptance as their king and then do as he pleased when he became their king. The Chronicler sharpened the statement to mean that only by being compassionate and conciliatory would Rehoboam forever win their hearts.

In reporting Rehoboam's answer to the elders of the ten tribes, the Chronicler explained that Rehoboam's hard line toward the ten tribes was brought about by God to fulfill the prophetic word of Ahijah the Shilonite to Jeroboam the son of Nebat concerning the division of the united Hebrew kingdom (vv. 12-15). Accordingly, the ten tribes of Israel rejected the rule of Rehoboam, leaving Rehoboam to reign only over the people of Israel who dwelt in the cities of Judah (vv. 16-17). Rehoboam, however, attempted to continue his reign upon the ten tribes of Israel by sending Hadoram, his chief taskmaster, to exact labor quotas from them (v. 18a). But the ten tribes stoned to death the chief taskmaster, and Rehoboam himself fled for his life from Shechem to Jerusalem (vv. 18b-19). Although the Chronicler sought to idealize Solomon, his reference to the prophetic word of Ahijah concerning the division of the kingdom speaks loud and clear concerning Solomon's apostasy for those who want to hear.

Establishment of His Reign over Judah (11:1-23)

Rehoboam returned to Jerusalem and assembled an army to whip the northern tribes into submission (v. 1). However, God by the mouth of Shemaiah his prophet told Rehoboam not to go to war to restore to his kingdom the ten tribes of Israel (vv. 2-4a), and Rehoboam obeyed (v. 4b).

Verses 5-23 describe the steps by which Rehoboam was firmly entrenched as king of Judah. First, Rehoboam built fortified cities in Judah and Benjamin to secure his kingdom (vv. 5-12). These fortified cities gave Judah protection from the Egyptians to the south and the Philistines to the west.

Second, the Kingdom of Judah was strengthened morally and therefore nationally by the godly influence of the Levites and other true worshipers who migrated to Judah from the ten tribes of Israel (vv. 13-17). The Levites were the legitimate priests and teachers of the law of God. However, the worship of the Lord under the symbol of the golden calves, which was instituted as a state religion in Northern Israel by Jeroboam the son of Nebat, left no place for the genuine Levites. "Satyrs," which commonly refers to goats, were idols of wild animals or demons with goatlike features used for licentious worship (Lev. 17:7). The brutal and lustful nature of these pagan gods doubtless inspired the worshipers to heinous deeds. For the nature of calf worship, see commentary on 1

Kings 12:25-33. Rather than give up their holy calling, the Levites left the cities assigned to them by Moses and Joshua and settled in Judah where they could continue their work without hindrance. They were accompanied by lay people who also were totally devoted to the true worship of God as found in the law of Moses (v. 16). These immigrants gave Rehoboam security for three years (17); however, at the end of that time, their godly influence was either overcome by the apostasy of the king and the people or these godly immigrants were themselves polluted by the apostasy. "In the way of . . . Solomon" once again idealizes Solomon.

Verses 18-23 describe Rehoboam's family and some of his activities toward them. As a third step for strengthening his reign, he wisely deployed throughout Judah and Benjamin some of his sons to maintain his influence and to guard against disloyalty.

His Abandonment of the Lord and Consequential Judgment (12:1-12)

Rehoboam followed at least superficially in the way of the Lord for the first years of his reign. However, when he was firmly established as king, he forsook the Lord. "All Israel" (v. 1) refers to the Israelites of Judah and Benjamin who now constituted true Israel as viewed by the Chronicler. Accordingly, both the Northern and Southern Kingdoms stood corrupted before God. See commentary on 1 Kings 14:21-31 for the grievous nature of Rehoboam's sin.

The promised judgment by which God would chasten his faithless people was not slow in coming. In the fifth year of Rehoboam's reign, King Shishak of Egypt invaded Judah, conquered all of their fortified cities, and came to the very gate of Jerusalem where Rehoboam and the princes of Judah huddled in desperation (vv. 2-4). Upon hearing from the mouth of Shemaiah the prophet that God had put Judah in the hands of Shishak because of their abandoning him, they repented (vv. 5-6). Accordingly, God moderated his wrath upon them (vv. 7-12). He decided not to destroy Rehoboam and Judah (v. 7). However, he would make Rehoboam and Judah the servants of Shishak to teach them how much better it is to enjoy the blessings of serving the Lord (v. 8). Their servitude to Shishak resulted in his taking everything from the treasures of the house of God and the treasures of the king's house including the shields of gold Solomon had made to decorate the House of the Forest of Lebanon (9:16). Thereafter Rehoboam and his people enjoyed relief from Shishak and prosperity to the degree that Rehoboam humbled himself before the Lord (vv. 10-12).

Analysis and Conclusion of Rehoboam's Reign (12:13-16)

After a summary statement of Rehoboam's reign (v. 13a), the Chronicler noted the age at which Rehoboam began to reign (v. 13b), the length of his reign (v. 13c), his mother's name (v. 13d), and his evil heart (v. 14). He also noted other sources of Rehoboam's reign (v. 15a), the continuous wars between Rehoboam and Jeroboam the king of Northern Israel (v. 15b), and Rehoboam's death, burial, and successor (v. 16).

The Reign of Abijah (13:1-22)

This section includes an introductory summary of Abijah's reign (vv. 1-2), a description of his war with Jeroboam the king of northern Israel (vv. 3-21), and a source of additional information on Abijah's reign (v. 22). See comments on 1 Kings 15:1 for the significance of the name Abijah and of his alternate name Abijam.

The Chronicler in his purpose to show the best side of the kings of Judah omitted references to Abijah's sin. Note commentary on 1 Kings 15:1-8 to see: (1) that Abijah deepened the religious apostasy of Solomon and of Rehoboam in also following the Canaanite fertility practices; and (2) that God's steadfast love toward David alone kept him from removing Abijah from the throne and destroying Jerusalem and the people.

Also true to his purpose to provide additional materials in relation to the kings of Judah, the Chronicler gave details of Northern Israel, to which the author of Kings only alluded (vv. 3-21; 1 Kings 15:6). The Chronicler first noted the drawing of the battle line (v. 3). Next he reported Abijah's inspired speech to Jeroboam and to all Israel (vv. 4-12). Although the exact location of "Mount Zemaraim" is uncertain, it was in the hill country of Ephraim, probably a little south of Bethel on the border of Judah and Israel. In his speech, Abijah declared that Jeroboam and the ten tribes over which he ruled were withstanding "the kingdom of God in the hand of the sons of David" (v. 8) in failing to submit themselves to his rule. Specifically, Abijah declared that Judah alone had remained true to God's everlasting covenant with David in following the house of David, had continued the true worship of God as given by Moses, and as such were the people with God at their head. "Salt," because of its preserving qualities, symbolized a lasting covenant. "O sons of Israel, do not fight against the Lord" (v. 12) was more than a warning of sure defeat. It was also an appeal for Jeroboam and the ten tribes to submit themselves to the rule of the house of David. In spite of Jeroboam's troop superiority and his well-executed ambush (vv. 3,13-14), "God defeated Jeroboam and all Israel before Abijah and Judah" (v. 15). Even though Abijah was not true in his worship of the Lord, God gave him and Judah the victory "because they relied upon the Lord, the God of their fathers" (v. 18), whereas Jeroboam relied on his troop superiority and the gods of his own devising (vv. 8-9). Abijah's victory was so decisive that Jeroboam did not recover his power during the days of Abijah (v. 20a). Moreover, God afflicted unto death Jeroboam for his continued rebellion against the true worship of God. Although how Jeroboam died is not told, "and the Lord smote him" (v. 20) often is used of sudden death (1 Sam. 25:38; Ex. 12:29). See commentary on 1 Kings 11:29-37 for the conditional promises of God to Jeroboam by which God would have established the dynasty of Jeroboam over Northern Israel for the total time of the affliction upon the house of David. Abijah was blessed for the sake of David rather than for himself (v. 21; 1 Kings 15:4-5).

The Reign of Asa (14:1 to 16:14)

Fortunately for Judah, the wicked but comparatively short reigns of Rehoboam and Abijah (twenty years total) were followed by the long and godly reigns of Asa and of his son Jehoshaphat, who ruled respectively forty-one years and twenty-five years (1 Kings 15:10; 2 Chron. 20:31). One reason Judah continued to endure as a nation is because from time to time godly kings such as Asa and Jehoshaphat led their nation back to God. In keeping with his desire to magnify the blessings of God lavished upon those kings who honored the house of God, the Chronicler greatly expanded the treatment given to the reign of Asa found in the Kings material (1 Kings 15:9-24). However, rather than gloss over Asa's evil as he had done in the cases of Solomon, Rehoboam, and Abijah, the Chronicler noted deviations in Asa's life from perfect faith in the Lord (2 Chron. 16:7-9).

His Early Reign (14:1-8)

"The land had rest for ten years" (v. 1) during the early years of Asa's reign because of his personal loyalty to the Lord his God and because of the religious reforms he instituted in coming to the throne (vv. 2-5). For an understanding of "the foreign altars" and "the high places." "pillars," and "Asherim," see commentary on 1 Kings 3:1-3; 11:1-8; 14:21-24; and 16:30-33. The Chronicler noted that Asa both "took out of all the cities of Judah the high places" (v. 5) and failed to take out "the high places . . . out of Israel" (15:17). Apparently what happened is that he ordered and sought to enforce the removal of these country shrines that were built after the manner of Canaanite altars, but were used for the worship of the Lord. Although blameless in his effort (15:17), he did not succeed, so that it must be said in the final analysis that "the high places were not taken away" (1 Kings 15:14). "Because we have sought the Lord" (v. 7) reflects Asa's understanding that their continuance in the Land as a nation depended on their obedience to God. His seeking the Lord gave him wisdom to fortify the cities of Judah and to get a strong standing army (vv. 7-8). Being both godly and militarily prepared, "they . . . prospered."

His God-given Victory over the Ethiopians (14:9-15)

Some interpreters take the term "million" to be figurative for "impossible to number." "Mareshah" (v. 10), where Asa intercepted the Ethiopians, was located in the lowlands of Judah not too far from Gath. Perhaps, it is to be identified with "Moresheth-gath," the likely home of Micah the prophet (Mic. 1:1,14). In response to Asa's prayer, the Lord gave Judah a mighty victory that included the overthrow of the Ethiopians in the initial battle (v. 12), the slaughter of the fleeing Ethiopians (vv. 13-14a), and the return of the victorious army of Judah with much booty (v. 14b).

His Desire for Godly Living Inspired by the Preaching of Azariah (15:1-19)

This passage illustrates the power of men of God to inspire kings, presidents, and other leaders to godly living. Azariah, whose name means, "the Lord has helped," encouraged Asa to press continued godly reforms in the Land so the Lord would continue to help him and his nation. The basic idea of "spirit" is to breathe or blow. "The Spirit of God" (v. 1), accordingly, denotes the animating force of God by which he enabled his prophets boldly and accurately to speak his word even to providing predictive messages that were later fulfilled. Many interpreters see "the Spirit of God" as referring to God himself coming in the power of the Holy Spirit upon the prophet and, thus, would translate it "the Spirit of God." Note 2 Chronicles 20:14. "And he went out to meet Asa" (v. 2) indicates that Azariah met and delivered his message to Asa as Asa returned to Jerusalem from his great God-given victory over the enormous Ethiopian army (v. 11).

His message, which was addressed to all of the people as well as to Asa (v. 2*a*), had three points. First, he declared that the Lord would be with Asa and with all Judah and Benjamin as long as they were loyal to him (v. 2*b*). Second, he used the history of Israel to illustrate that forsaking the Lord leads to tragedy and national defeat, but faithfulness to the Lord leads to blessings and national victory (vv. 3-6). "Without the true God, and without a teaching priest, and without law" describes the era of the judges when the people brought spiritual famine upon themselves by their forsaking God. Note Judges 3:7 to 5:31 to observe the oft-repeated cycle of apostasy, punishment, seeking God's face, restoration and prosperity through a delivering judge, and then apostasy, and so forth to repeat the cycle. Third, he exhorted Asa and promised him reward for continuing to do the work of God (v. 7). "But you" (v. 7), literally, "but as for you," is a strong, personal appeal for Asa himself to learn from history.

Asa did take courage from the preaching of Azariah and continued to press godly reforms throughout all of the land over which he had control, which included the land of Judah and Benjamin and the cities he had taken from Northern Israel in the hill country of Ephraim (v. 8*a*). Specifically, he purged the land of idols (v. 8*b*), repaired the great altar of the house of the Lord (v. 8*c*), led the people into a covenant to seek the Lord with all their heart and soul (vv. 9-15), removed his grandmother from being queen mother because of her idolatry (v. 16*a*), and destroyed her pagan image (v. 16*b*). Also, Asa desposited in the treasury of the house of God the free-will gifts of his father and of himself (v. 18). The results of his godly reforms were twofold: (1) he and the people found the Lord; and (2) they prospered without war until Asa's thirty-fifth year of reign (vv. 15*c*,19). Asa, thus, learned from history to trust in God and to prosper. But regrettably, he did not learn to continue in the ways of God.

His War with Baasha and Reliance upon Ben-hadad for Security (16:1-6).

Asa had a spiritual lapse in his thirty-sixth year of reign which continued until his death in the forty-first year of his reign (16:1-14). The implication is that Asa's war with Baasha the king of northern Israel came to chastise Asa for his spiritual lapse and to provide the background for the miraculous deliverance that would bring Asa back to God. However, instead of turning to God as he had done in the case of the Ethiopian crisis in his early reign (15:11), Asa relied on alliances with Ben-hadad king of Syria for his security (16:1-6).

His Rebuke and Prophecy of Continued Wars by Hanani the Seer (16:7-10)

Immediately, Hanani the seer rebuked Asa for his lack of faith in God and prophesied continued wars for Asa and his people instead of the security and prosperity God would have given. "The army of the king of Syria has escaped you" (v. 7) suggests that Asa could have conquered Syria as well as Northern Israel had he trusted in God. Accordingly, by trust in God, Asa could have united the divided kingdom and extended its borders to include the nation of Syria! "For the eyes of the Lord run to and fro" (v. 9) means that God, the keeper of those who trust him, stands by eagerly awaiting opportunity to help those who are "blameless toward him." "Blameless," with its root idea of completeness, does not mean sinless, but completely dedicated to God. Instead of repenting of his sin, Asa sought to silence the prophet by putting him in prison (v. 10a). "Inflicted cruelties upon some of the people" (v. 10b) indicates that Asa also persecuted at that time some of Hanani's followers who doubtless objected to Asa's putting the prophet into prison.

Conclusion (16:11-14)

Asa's rebellion against God continued until the time of his death. Some interpreters think that tactlessness on Hanani's part contributed to the hardness of Asa's heart. In any case, the man of God should speak the truth with love (Eph. 4:15). Even the severe disease in his feet, which could have been caused from circulatory problems rooted in something like diabetes, failed to turn Asa back to God. No information is given as to whether the disease, like the wars (16:6), was in punishment for his sin. Asa was not condemned for consulting physicians, but for seeking help from them apart from God (v. 12). Medicine and faith are not in opposition to one another. Physicians of the right sort are one of God's gifts to men, and even prophets like Isaiah often used medicine to heal (2 Kings 20:7). The problem was Asa's stubborn refusal to seek the help of God. "A very great fire" (v. 14b) was required to burn the large number of perfumed spices prepared for his honor. His body was embalmed and placed in his tomb in keeping with the customs of the Middle East (v. 14a).

The Reign of Jehoshaphat (17:1 to 21:1)

The Chronicler, in contrast with the author of Kings (1 Kings 22:41-50), gave extensive treatment to the reign of good king Jehoshaphat. The obvious reason is that Jehoshaphat was devoted to the Lord and to his house more than any king of Judah except Hezekiah and Josiah. His major contribution was in continuing to press the godly reforms initiated by Asa his father. Their total reigns of sixty-six years swept back the floodtide of wickedness that engulfed the life of Judah because of the wicked reigns of Solomon (his last days), Rehoboam, and Abijah. The commentary on 1 Kings 22:41-50 demonstrates that his biggest mistake was in making alliances with the kings of Israel. His reign of twenty-five years overlapped the reigns of three kings of Israel—of Ahab for eighteen years, of Azariah (Ahab's son) for two years, and of Jehoram (also Ahab's son) for five years.

His Establishment in His Kingdom by the Lord (17:1-6)

Once again personal godliness is seen to have resulted in wisdom for achieving military preparedness. Jehoshaphat strengthened himself against Northern Israel by placing forces in all fortified cities that Asa and other kings of Judah had built (vv. 1-2). The Lord was with Jehoshaphat because Jehoshaphat followed the earlier example of his father Asa in seeking the Lord (vv. 3-4). As the result of Jehoshaphat's seeking the Lord, the Lord established Jehoshaphat's kingdom (v. 5a), all Judah brought tribute to Jehoshaphat (v. 5b), and Jehoshaphat had great riches and honor (v. 5c). His seeking the Lord also increased his courage so that he took steps to remove "the high places and the Asherim out of Judah" (v. 6). "Asherim," the plural of Asherah, were wooden symbols of the goddess Asherah who was the consort of Baal. See commentary on 1 Kings 16:29-34. "The high places" were country Canaanite shrines that had been adapted for the worship of the Lord. See commentary on 1 Kings 3:1-3. "He took the high places . . . out of Judah" (v. 6) probably means that he issued royal decrees to abolish these shrines, but that the people refused to obey (1 Kimgs 22:43; 2 Chron. 20:33). He may have been successful in removing the shrines immediately in and around Jerusalem.

His Teaching the People the Law of the Lord (17:7-9)

The Chronicler noted the time of his teaching mission (v. 7a), the princely leaders of his teaching mission (v. 7b), the Levitical leaders of his teaching mission (v. 8a), the priestly leaders of his teaching mission (v. 8b), and the scope of their teaching (v. 9b). Most likely the priests and other Levites taught "the book of the law of the Lord," that is, the law of Moses. The princes made certain that the people assembled to hear the teachers.

His Security, Wealth, Military Strength, and Honor (17:10-19)

Other nations, recognizing that God was with Jehoshaphat, made no war with Jehoshaphat, but brought him tribute (vv. 10-11). Therefore, Jehoshaphat grew steadily greater (v. 12a) and was able to build additional fortresses in Judah (v. 12b), to build and fill up in Judah great store-cities (vv. 12c-13a), and to maintain a great army (vv. 13b-19).

His Unwise Alliance with Ahab King of Israel (18:1 to 19:3)

The Chronicler first alluded to Jehoshaphat's unwise marriage alliance with Ahab and Jezebel by which his son Jehoram married their daughter Athaliah (18:1;2 Kings 8:18). See commentary on 1 Kings 22:41-50. Second, the Chronicler described Jehoshaphat's ill-fated military campaign with King Ahab against the Syrians (18:2-34). With the slight variations in 18:2 and 18:34, the Chronicler's account of Jehoshaphat's military alliance with Ahab against Syria is the same as 1 Kings 22:1-36. See commentary on 1 Kings 22:1-40 for an interpretation of the reason for Ahab's war with Ben-hadad of Syria, the location and significance of Ramoth-gilead, and especially of the character and role of the true prophet Micaiah the son of Imlah in contrast with the other four hundred prophets of the Lord.

His Rebuke From God for His Wicked Alliances (19:1-3)

Jehoshaphat, who barely escaped death in the battle against Syria, returned in safety to his house in Jerusalem (v. 1). Jehu the son of Hanani the seer confronted Jehoshaphat with God's message of rebuke and wrath (v.2). However, Jehu moderated the word of judgment in speaking of the good in Jehoshaphat that led to his destroying the worship of Asherah and setting his heart to seek God (v. 3). His personal goodness resulted in God's general blessings upon him during the days of his reign. However, his children experienced the terrible wrath of God. In Jehoshaphat's case, the wrath of God was the natural outworking of the wickedness he had pulled to his bosom in embracing "those who hate the Lord" (v. 2). Under the wicked influence of Athaliah, the daughter of Ahab and Jezebel, his son Jehoram murdered his brothers and other rivals to the throne (2 Chron. 21:4), led the people of Judah into unfaithfulness for which they experienced a plague (2 Chron. 21:13-14), and experienced death by a severe intestinal disease (2 Chron. 21:15). Also, Athaliah's wickedness resulted in his grandson's evil reign and violent death (2 Chron. 22:1-9), in the near annihilation of the house of David (2 Chron. 22:10-11), and in the people's forsaking the house of God and returning to the worship of Asherim and related idols for which they experienced wrath (2 Chron. 24:17-19).

His Religious and Judicial Reforms (19:4-11)

Jehoshaphat apparently responded well to God's message of rebuke. He continued personally to bring the people back to God (v. 4). "From Beer-sheba to the hill country of Ephraim" describes respectively the southern and northern limits of his kingdom. His method in bringing the people back to God was threefold: (1) his continuation of the teaching mission by which the people understood the law of Moses (vv. 4,10; 17:7-9); (2) his establishment of district courts in strategic cities to govern the people according to the law of Moses (vv. 5-7); and (3) his appointment of a court of appeals in Jerusalem to decide hard cases (vv. 8-11). His exhortation to the judges concerning faithful performances of their duty shows them to be representatives of God who themselves stood under the higher judgment of God (vv. 6,7,11d).

His God-given Victory Over the Moabites, Ammonites, and Me-unites (20:1-30).

This account differs from the war with Moab described in 1 Kings 3:4-27. That war was an attack of Moab by Jehoram the son of Ahab to regain for Israel rebellious Moab for which Jehoram enlisted Jehoshaphat's help. In the case of this war, the coalition of the Moabites, Ammonites, and Me-unites attacked Judah from the south (vv. 1-2). The Chronicler first described Jehoshaphat's reaction to the attack (vv. 3-12). He feared (v. 3a), set himself to seek the Lord (v. 3b), and proclaimed a fast throughout all Judah (v. 3c). Apparently, the fast also involved the assembling of the people at the house of God to pray for deliverance in accord with God's promise to Solomon to give them victory in their humbly and penitentially praying for help to God in his house (2 Chron. 6:23-31,34-35). Accordingly, Jehoshaphat stood among the assembled people in the house of God and prayed for deliverance (vv. 4-12). In his prayer Jehoshaphat declared God's ability to help them (v. 6); referred to God's past exploits in giving them the Land (v. 7); claimed God's special promise of victory (vv. 8-9); declared to God that they had in no way provoked the invaders (vv. 10-11); asked God to execute judgment upon the invaders (v. 12a); admitted that unless God helped them they were powerless to stand against the invaders (v. 12b); and announced that they did not know what to do, but they looked to the Lord for guidance (v. 12c).

True to his promise, the Lord acted to give them victory (vv. 13-25).

First, the Spirit of the Lord came upon Jehaziel to announce the forth-coming miraculous victory (vv. 13-17). The only thing the people were to do was to positionize themselves to observe the great victory God would give. In response to this announcement, Jehoshaphat and his people bowed in worship of God and the Levites stood up to praise God (vv. 18-19). The next day, the king and the people obediently went out to assume their appointed positions, with the king encouraging them to believe in the Lord and in his prophets (v. 20). The king, in counsel with the people, assigned those who would go before the army to sing praises to God (v. 21). As the people began to sing, the Lord ambushed and destroyed the invading army by turning them against one another in battle (vv. 22-23). The king and the people beheld the greatness of the victory and spent the three days necessary to collect the spoils of victory (vv. 24-25). In conclusion, the king and the people assembled on the fourth day in the Valley of Beracah (blessing), to bless the Lord for his great victory (v. 26). Then they returned in triumph to the house of God in Jerusalem with joy and praise and musical celebration (vv. 27-28). Because God gave his people such a miraculous victory, great fear came upon all of Judah's neighbors, resulting in peace for Jehoshaphat and his people (vv. 29-30).

Concluding Notations on Jehoshaphat's Reign (20:31 to 21:1)

Included in this section are a summary and characterization of his reign (20:31-34), a report on his wicked maritime partnership with Ahaziah king of Israel (20:35-37), and statements concerning his death, burial, and successor (21:1). The destruction of Jehoshaphat's fleet was an outworking of God's wrath upon Jehoshaphat for his sin of joining himself in partnership with wicked Ahaziah the son of Ahab and king of Northern Israel. In this case, God's wrath was seemingly a deliberate stroke of judgment by which the fleet was destroyed.

The Reign of Jehoram (21:2-20)

In contrast with the lengthy treatment of good king Jehoshaphat, the Chronicler gave brief treatment to the wicked reign of Jehoram the son and successor of Jehoshaphat. As has been noted, the reign of Jehoram illustrates the folly of Jehoshaphat's marriage alliance with wicked King Ahab and Queen Jezebel by which his son Jehoram took their daughter Athaliah for wife.

His Slaughter of Possible Opposition (21:2-4)

The Chronicler named Jehoram's brothers (v. 2), Jehoshaphat's gifts to his sons including the kingdom to Jehoram his firstborn (v. 3), and noted Jehoram's murder of his brothers and other possible rivals for the throne (v. 4).

Summary of his Reign (21:5-7)

Inspired by his wicked wife Athaliah, Jehoram walked in the evil "way of the kings of Israel, as the house of Ahab had done" (v. 6a). This probably means that he followed Ahab in the practices of both calf worship and Baalism. God withheld the deserved punishment that would have destroyed Judah as a nation only because of his commitment to David to give him a son forever upon the throne of David in Jerusalem (v. 7).

Successful Revolt of Edom and Libnah (21:8-10)

The Chronicler first described the revolt of Edom (vv. 8-10a) and then that of Libnah (v. 10b). "Also revolted . . . because" indicates that both of these successful revolts, which weakened the kingdom of Judah, were the result of God's punishment upon wicked Jehoram.

His Wicked Influence (21:11)

"High places" made by Jehoram seem to be in addition to his promotion of the calf worship and Baalism, the specific sins of Northern Israel. See commentary on 1 Kings 3:1-3 for "high places," 1 Kings 12:25-33 for calf worship, and 1 Kings 16:29-34 for Baalism. In any case, he led by his wicked influence Judah and the inhabitants of Jerusalem into unfaithfulness (v. 11b).

His Judgment Letter from Elijah the Prophet (21:12-15).

Elijah the prophet sent Jehoram a letter in which he enumerated Jehoram's sin (vv. 12-13) and pronounced judgment upon Jehoram for his sin (vv. 14-15). Elijah, who actively served in the Northern Kingdom during the reigns of Ahab and his sons Ahaziah and Jehoram, seemingly had been succeeded by Elisha as the prophet after the first days of Jehoram's reign (1 Kings 3:11). Elijah may have sent the letter to Jehoram rather than appearing personally because he was infirm by this time. Some interpreters suggest that Elijah had already died, but reappeared to dictate this letter to an unnamed prophet for him to deliver. Elijah's predicted judgment upon Jehoram would come as God brought: (1) a great plague upon Jehoram's people, his children, his wives, and all of his possessions (v. 14); and (2) a disintegrating disease upon Jehoram's bowels (v. 15).

Fulfillment of the Judgment Letter (21:16-20)

To fulfill the predicted plague, God stirred up the Philistines and the Arabs to pillage Jehoram's possessions, sons, and wives (vv. 16-17). Only Jehoahaz, his youngest, was left of his sons. His wife Athaliah, the daughter of Ahab and Jezebel, likewise escaped death at the hands of the marauders. Also, God smote Jehoram with an incurable disease of the bowels, which resulted at the end of two years in total disintegration of his bowels and his agonizing death (vv. 18-19a). Jehoram also was dishonored by the people of Judah at his death (vv. 19b-20). Three facts point up his dishonor among the people at death. "No fire in his honor" means no incense burning. See 16:14. "No one's regret" means that no one regretted his passing, that is, desired for him to live on. He was not buried in the tombs of the kings lest his dishonorable body corrupt their bones.

The Reign of Ahaziah (22:1-9)

His Establishment on the Throne by the Inhabitants of Jerusalem (22:1)

At the death of his disease-smitten father, Ahaziah was established on the throne of Judah by the inhabitants of Jerusalem. Ahaziah, also known as Jehoahaz (21:17), was the youngest and only surviving son of Jehoram and Athaliah. The massacre of the king's sons by the marauding Philistines and Arabs probably occasioned the unusual action by which the people of Jerusalem themselves crowned Ahaziah as king. Some interpreters suggest that there was a struggle for the crown between Ahaziah and his mother Athaliah, who usurped the crown after his death. But his following his mother's counsel as well as that of the house of Ahab implies good relations between them.

General Characterization of His Reign (22:2-4)

"Forty-two years old when he began to reign" (v. 2) should probably read "twenty-two" (2 Kings 8:26). "Forty-two" would make Ahaziah two years old at his father's birth (21:5). The evil reign and violent death of Ahaziah, the grandson of Jehoshaphat, after one year upon the throne is another example of the tragic results of Jehoshaphat's unholy alliance with the house of Omri/Ahab by which Athaliah, the daughter of Ahab and Jezebel, came into the royal family of David. The Chronicler spelled out the wicked influence of Athaliah and the house of Ahab upon Ahaziah that was implied in the Kings material (2 Kings 8:26-27). Athaliah's wickedness went back to her grandfather Omri, who founded their evil house. She and her wicked house inspired Ahaziah to do evil, just as they had inspired wickedness in Jehoram her husband (21:6) and just as her mother Jezebel had inspired to evil her father Ahab (1 Kings 21:25-26). "To his undoing" (v. 4), as viewed from the total biblical perspective, means more than an evil reign and violent death. Included also would be the eternal destruction experienced by those who reject God and his salvation.

His Military Alliance with Jehoram King of Israel (22:5-6)

The wicked counsel of Athaliah and others of the house of Ahab also resulted in Ahaziah's unwise alliance with Jehoram the king of Northern Israel against Hazael, king of Syria. This alliance explained how Ahaziah happened to be visiting Jehoram at Jezreel where Ahaziah met his violent death at the hands of Jehu, God's avenger.

His Providential Death at the Hands of Jehu the Son of Nimshi (vv. 22:7-9)

See commentary on 1 Kings 21:19-24 and 2 Kings 9:1-10 for God's commission of Jehu as his avenger to destroy the house of Ahab. "The princes of Judah" were not royal seed, but court officials who served as teachers and guardians of the royal seed. The executions of Ahaziah, his princes, and the sons of his brothers were within the commission of Jehu, since they were grandsons and great-grandsons of Ahab. See commentary on 2 Kings 8:25-29. For certain details concerning the death and burial of Ahaziah, see commentary on 2 Kings 9:27-28. "And the house of Ahaziah had no one able to rule the kingdom" sets the stage for Athaliah's violent usurpation of the throne of David.

The Reign of Athaliah (22:10 to 23:21)

Very little attention is actually given to the events of the six-year reign of Athaliah, who usurped the throne of Judah. Although Athaliah ruled in name, the real ruler through whom God kept alive the light of David on the throne in Jerusalem was Joash the son of Ahaziah. The Chronicler focused on Athaliah's murder of all of the royal seed except baby Joash (22:10-12). Then he skipped over the events of her reign to the crowning of Joash as king (23:1-11), to the slaughter of Athaliah

(23:12-15), and finally to the religious reformation led by Jehoiada the priest (23:16-21).

Her Murder of All of the Royal Seed Except the Baby Joash (22:10-12)

"The royal family of the house of Judah" (v. 10) refers to the royal descendants of David that remained after the pillage of the royal family by the Arabs and the Philistines and after Jehu's slaughter of Ahaziah and his kinsmen (21:16-17; 22:7-9; 2 Kings 10:13-14). "The king's sons" (v. 11) would be the sons of Ahaziah by all of his wives and concubines, all of whom were grandsons of the wicked Athaliah. Her near annihilation of the descendants of David is another example of the tragic results of the unholy alliance of Jehoshaphat with the house of Ahab. "Jehoshabe-ath" is a variation of the name "Jehosheba" (2 Kings 11:2). She was the daughter of King Jehoram, probably by some wife other than Athaliah and, thus, the half-sister of King Ahaziah. She also was the wife of Jehoiada the priest (v. 11). Apparently, she represented the seething discontent of the godly people with the evil introduced into Judah by Athaliah and others of the house of Ahab. Her rescue of the child Joash was the providential preservation of the descendants of David.

The Crowning of Joash as King (23:1-11)

In this section the Chronicler noted: the pact to make Joash king (vv. 1-4); the plans for protecting Joash and the Temple (vv. 5-7); and the presentation of Joash as king (vv. 8-11). A comparison of this section with 2 Kings 11:4-12 reflects the purpose of the Chronicler both to supplement the Kings material and also to magnify the role of the Levites. The Kings material, for example, is silent about the role of the Levites (except Jehoiada) in crowning Joash. In addition to the commanders of the royal bodyguard, the Chronicler noted that Jehoiada enlisted the help of the Levites from all the cities of Judah and also the heads of fathers' houses of Israel (v. 2). The Chronicler also added to the Kings material the steps taken by the priests and other Levites not to defile the house of God with unclean people as well as the blood of Athaliah (vv. 6,14; 2 Kings 11:15). See commentary on 2 Kings 11:4-16 for the meaning of "the crown" and "the testimony." Note comments on 1 Kings 1:28-40 for the meaning of "anointing."

The Slaughter of Athaliah (23:12-15)

Athaliah went to the house of God upon hearing the noise of the people "running and praising the king" (v. 12). There she saw the king standing "by his pillar" and recognized the treason against her (v. 13). Then she was executed (vv. 14-15). "His pillar" was either Jachin or Boaz, which was the place designated for the king to stand in worship before God and the people (2 Kings 23:3). See commentary on 1 Kings 7:13-51 for the significance of the names of the pillars. Executing Athaliah at "the horse gate of the king's house" (v. 15) seemingly has no significance other than being a place outside of the Temple area.

The Reformation Led by Jehoiada the Priest (23:16-21)

This section reports on steps immediately taken by Jehoiada to turn the nation back to the true worship of the Lord God of Israel. First, he made a covenant between himself, all of the people, and the king to be God's people. Note commentary on 1 Kings 11:17-20 to see that this actually was a twofold covenant. On the one hand, the king and the people committed themselves to live by the law of God. On the other hand, the king committed himself to rule the people by the law of God and the people pledged themselves to obey him as the God-appointed ruler. Second, to implement this covenant, the people tore down the house of Baal and executed the priest of Baal (v. 17). The execution of the priest of Baal was in keeping with the requirement of the Mosaic law to destroy false prophets from the land (Deut. 17:2-7; 1 Kings 18:40). Third, Jehoiada reestablished worship in the Temple according to the law of Moses and the ordinance of David (vv. 18-19). Finally, he enthroned Joash as the God-appointed king (vv. 20-21).

The Reign of Joash (24:1-27)

The Chronicler gave rather limited treatment to the reign of Joash, doubtless because Joash was limited in his devotion to the Lord God of Israel. The good work for which Joash is praised was his repair of the Temple. Notice that in this short chapter the expression "the house of the Lord" or its equivalent is used fifteen times (vv. 4,5,7, and so forth).

Characterization of His Reign and Family Relationships (24:1-3)

Joash did right in the eyes of God as long, but only as long, as Jehoiada lived. See commentary on 2 Kings 11:21 to 12:21 for limitations in Joash's ministry as a godly king. The two wives chosen for young Joash by Jehoiada his regent, although many less than the numerous

wives of David and Solomon, was in violation of the injunction for a
king not to multiply wives (Deut. 17:7).

His Restoration of the House of the Lord and Its Services (24:4-14)

Joash's work in restoring the house of the Lord and its services was in
addition to the reforms of Jehoiada at the time Joash was enthroned as
king (23:16-21). Jehoiada reinstituted the worship services that had been
neglected under the wicked influence of Athaliah and the house of Ahab.
Joash physically repaired the Temple that had been broken down and
pillaged by the equally wicked sons of Athaliah (v. 7). The Chronicler
noted in this section: (1) Joash's determination to restore the house of the
Lord (v. 4); (2) his command to the priests and other Levites to have all
of the people bring in the tax levied by Moses for the repair of the Temple
(vv. 5-7); (3) the execution of the tax command at the insistence of Joash
by which money was provided for restoration and the repairs were accomplished (vv. 8-14a); and (4) that services were carried out in the
house of the Lord all the days of Jehoiada (v. 14b). See commentary on 2
Kings 11:21 to 12:21 for an interpretation of Joash's plan for the repair
of the Temple and his conflict with the priests in executing the plan.

The Death of Jehoiada (24:15-16)

The Chronicler noted the death of Jehoiada (v. 15a), his age at death
(v. 15b), and his burial and honor (v. 16). The burial of Jehoiada in the
city of David among the kings (the royal cemetery) was in recognition of
the good he had done "in Israel, and toward God and his house" (v. 16).
Among his good works were his saving the life and throne of Joash, his
saving the royal descendants of David, his execution of wicked Athaliah,
his purging the land of idolatry, his restoration of true worship in the
Land, his repair of the house of God, and his influence on Joash to walk
in the ways of the Lord.

His Turning from God After the Death of Jehoiada (24:17-18)

Here is another example of the tragic results of Jehoshaphat's unholy
alliance that brought the house of Ahab into the life of Judah. The evil
influence of Athaliah in introducing Baalism to the people of Judah lived
on! The princes of Judah and the people they represented wanted to return to this tantalizing, licentious worship. When Jehoiada was no
longer alive to lead Joash in the true way of God, he hearkened to their
evil influence (v. 17), joined them in turning from the house of God to
serve Asherim and idols (v. 18a), and thereby brought the wrath of God
upon Judah and Jerusalem (v. 18b).

His Unwillingness to Repent (24:19-22)

God moderated his wrath upon Joash, his princes, and his people in sending prophets to turn them from their sin (v. 19a). However, they would not heed the prophets (v. 19b). Indeed, Joash murdered Zechariah the son of Jehoiada whom God used in the effort to call them back to himself (vv. 20-23). The hardness of Joash in killing the son of the man who had saved and nurtured him illustrates the depths to which even a good man can be plunged by sin. He had Zechariah stoned to death for calling him back from the very sin from which he and Jehoiada had saved the nation years before. Moreover, Joash had him stoned in the court of the house of the Lord where he, Jehoiada, and the people had covenanted together to live according to the law of God. Zechariah's dying plea for God to see and avenge his murderer (v. 22) was soon to be answered.

His Providential Downfall (24:23-26)

The small army of the Syrians executed God's judgment upon Joash and his numerically superior army (v. 24). "The princes of the people" (v. 23) who encouraged Joash to turn from God back to the worship of Baal were destroyed, and Joash himself was severely wounded (v. 25a). Moreover, Joash's own servants brought the blood of the son of Jehoiada the priest on the head of Joash in their violently taking his life in his own bed (v. 25a). Joash was buried with his father only in the sense that his tomb was in the city of David (v. 25; 2 Kings 12:21). He was not buried in the royal cemetery.

Additional Sources for His Reign (24:27)

"Commentary" is the word *Midrash* in the Hebrew, whose basic meaning carries the ideas of seeking out and expounding upon. Accordingly, "the Commentary on the Book of the Kings" was a study and exposition of "the Book of Kings" much like a biblical commentary today. "The Book of Kings" may even be the canonical 1 and 2 Kings from which the Chronicler often drew material, many times even word-for-word.

The Reign of Amaziah (25:1-28)

Summary of His Reign (25:1-2)

This passage includes his age when he began to reign (v. 1a), the length of his reign (v. 1b), and the name of his mother (v. 1c). "Blameless" (v. 2), as noted in 16:9, has as its basic meaning wholeness and completeness. Accordingly, it carries the idea of completely dedicated. Rather than serve God with his whole heart, Amaziah followed in the limited way of Joash his father (v. 2).

His Vengeance upon His Father's Assassinators (25:3-4)

His sparing the children of those who assassinated his father Joash was in accord with the law of Moses, which specified that only those who committed the crime and not their families should be punished (Deut. 24:16). Note, however, the commentary on 2 Kings 14:1-22 to see that all of these killings, beginning with Joash's murder of Zechariah (24:25), would be judged as murders and not as civil executions authorized by the law of Moses.

His Campaign Against the Edomites (25:5-13)

As noted in the commentary on 2 Kings 14:1-22, Edom successfully revolted from Judah during the reign of Jehoram as part of God's punishment of that wicked king (2 Kings 8:20-22). Amaziah's campaign against the Edomites was intended to retake Edom. The Chronicler noted Amaziah's muster of his men of war (v. 5), his hiring of one hundred thousand mighty men of valor from Israel to strengthen his army (v. 6), his rebuke from the unnamed man of God for his alliance with the wicked forces of Israel (vv. 7-9), his discharge of the army of Israel (v. 10), his victory over the Edomites (vv. 11-12), and the abuse of Judah at the hands of the retiring army of Israel (v. 13). The man of God doubtless remembered the tragic results of Jehoshaphat's unholy alliance with the house of God. Note commentary on 2 Chronicles 18:1 to 19:3. The man of God insisted that Amaziah's including the mercenaries from Israel would be another unholy alliance that would result in Judah's defeat.

Amaziah's Defection from God and Silencing of the Rebuking Prophet (25:14-16)

Amaziah may have intended only to include the gods of the defeated Edomites among the gods that he served rather than to turn from God to them. His motive in including the gods of the Edomites would be to make the Edomites permanently subject to Judah by winning the favor of their gods by sacrificing to them. In any case, his worship of these gods was a violation of the covenant and incited immediate wrath from the Lord God of Israel and rebuke from his prophet (v. 15). Before the prophet stopped—at threat of death from Amaziah—he revealed that God had determined to destroy Amaziah for two reasons: (1) because he had embraced the gods of the Edomites; and (2) because he had refused to heed the advice of the prophet to put away these gods (v. 16). Amaziah's predicted destruction came at the hands of the Israelites who defeated him and Judah and even pillaged Jerusalem (vv. 20-24) and at the hands of conspirators who assassinated him (vv. 27-28).

His War with Joash the King of Israel (25:17-24)

Amaziah, encouraged by his victory over the Edomites, probably went to war against Joash (Jehoash, variant spelling) to avenge the pillage of the Judaean cities by the Israelite mercenaries. God, however, ordered the war to punish Amaziah for embracing the Edomite gods (v. 20). The Chronicler noted Amaziah's calling Joash out to battle (v. 17), his ridicule by Joash (vv. 18-19), his providential pursual of the war as punishment (vv. 20-21), his defeat and capture by Joash (vv. 22-23a), and Joash's pillage of Jerusalem (vv. 23b-24). See commentary on 2 Kings 14:1-22 for an interpretation of Joash's sarcastic analogy.

Conclusion of His Reign (25:25-28)

After Joash captured Amaziah and pillaged Jerusalem, he returned Amaziah to his throne in Jerusalem. In concluding his treatment of the reign of Amaziah, the Chronicler noted: (1) that Amaziah reigned fifteen years after the death of Joash the king of Israel (v. 25); (2) other sources of Amaziah's reign (v. 26); (3) his exile and death at the hands of conspirators to fulfill the prophecy concerning his destruction for embracing the Edomite gods (v. 27); and finally (4) his burial (v. 28).

The Reign of Uzziah (26:1-23)

Uzziah is prominent in the minds of Bible students because of his association with Isaiah the prophet who experienced his prophetic call in the year that King Uzziah died (Isa. 6:1). His reign of fifty-two years makes him second in longevity on the throne of Judah only to Manasseh, who reigned for fifty-five years. Chronicles gives more attention to the reign of Uzziah than does Kings. However, even the Chronicler is surprisingly brief in reporting the deeds of Uzziah. A probable reason was Uzziah's violation of the priestly office in his usurping the role of the priests (26:16).

General Observations Concerning His Reign (26:1-5)

Once again we have the unusual move of the people's rising up to crown a king (v. 1; 22:1). Their action was perhaps in reaction to the wickedness of the reign of Amaziah and in expression of their concern lest an older but wicked son of Amaziah should be made king. The Chronicler noted Uzziah's signal accomplishment in reconquering and constructing Eloth (Ezion-geber), which had been lost by Judah during the reign of Jehoram (21:8-10). For the significance of Eloth and its relationship to Ezion-geber, see commentery on 2 Chronicles 8:1-18. Uzziah is also called Azariah in Kings (2 Kings 15:1,13). The Chronicler probably used only the name Uzziah to distinguish the king from Azariah the priest (26:17) who is not mentioned in Kings. See commentary on 2 Kings 15:1-7 for significance of his name and that of his mother and for his half-hearted devotion to the Lord. Very little is known concerning Zechariah, who instructed Uzziah "in the fear of God" (v. 5). We are told that he had "understanding in the visions of God" (v. 5, KJV), which means that Zechariah had insight into the seeing of God. Doubtless Zechariah was gifted in the ability to lead men to understand and reverence the Lord God of Israel. As long as Uzziah was earnest in his effort to find and follow the Lord, God caused Uzziah to prosper (v. 5).

His Military Victories (26:6-8)

God's blessings upon Uzziah resulted in his military victories over the Philistines, the Arabs, the Me-unites, and the Ammonites. He consolidated his military victories by constructing "cities," most likely fortified cities, in the conquered territories. Jabneh, which is Jabneel of Joshua 15:11, was later known as Jamnia, the site where the Old Testament canon was debated and decided upon. Represented today by Yebna, it was located four miles inland from the Mediterranean about halfway between Joppa to the north and Ashkelon to the south.

His Internal Developments, Strength, and Fame (26:9-15)

God's blessings upon Uzziah led to progress in many areas. The Chronicler noted that Uzziah built towers to protect his herds from marauders in Jerusalem and in the wilderness (vv. 9-10a), hewed out cisterns to water his herds in the Shephelah and in the plain (v. 10b), had farmers and vinedressers in the hill country and other fertile areas suited for growing agricultural crops (v. 10c), and had a capable and well-equipped army (vv. 11-15a). Indeed, God's marvelous blessings continued upon Uzziah until he was strong and famous (15b). "Wilderness" (v. 10) usually refers to uninhabited tracts of land that could be used for pasturage such as the Judean hills. "Shephelah" (v. 10) refers to the lowlands along the Mediterranean Sea. "The plain" (v. 10) probably denotes the flat land east of the Jordan River from the Arnon River in the south to Heshbon in the north. "Engines" (v. 15) were war machines capable of shooting arrows or stones, apparently like the catapults used by the Romans.

His Pride, Sin, and Punishment with Leprosy (26:16-21)

Uzziah's strength led to pride, sin, and punishment. The basic idea in "proud" is to be lifted up. Accordingly, pride can be used in the good sense of one's boldly and courageously lifting up his head because of his full appreciation of his abilities, position, and so forth. It may, however, be used in the bad sense of one's arrogantly lifting up one's heart and head. "He grew proud" (v. 16) pictures Uzziah's arrogant exaltation of himself until he forgot who he was and God who had exalted him. His sin was threefold. First, he was "false to the Lord his God" (v. 16b). The basic idea in "false" is to act treacherously and unfaithfully. Uzziah betrayed God's trust in him, just as Benedict Arnold betrayed the trust of George Washington and the Colonies in 1780 in plotting to deliver West Point into the hands of the enemy. Second, he usurped in his arrogance the office of the priest in seeking to burn incense (v. 16c). Third, he refused to repent when stopped and rebuked by Azariah the high priest and the other priests (vv. 17-19a). See commentary on 2 Kings 15:1-7 to note that he probably would not have been punished with leprosy had he repented. "Destruction" (v. 16) may be too strong a word to describe his punishment with leprosy that continued (vv. 19b-21). The word itself means to cause to ruin or to spoil. Certainly, it spoiled the last days of his reign. See commentary on 2 Kings 15:1-7 for the results of his leprosy. God may have smitten his forehead with leprosy (v. 20) because his pride expressed itself in his lifting up his forehead.

Conclusion of His Reign (26:22-23)

The Chronicler noted an additional source of the acts of Uzziah (v. 22), his death (v. 23a), his burial (v. 23b), and his successor (v. 23c). See commentary on 2 Kings 15:1-7 for prophets in addition to Isaiah who served during Uzziah's long reign.

The Reign of Jotham (27:1-9)

Although Jotham was looked upon as a good king, he was not perfect in his devotion to the Lord and did not merit the praise of the Chronicler to the extent of Jehoshaphat, Hezekiah, and Josiah. He did, however, continue the work of his father Uzziah in providing security and prosperity for his people. The Chronicler made general observations concerning his reign (vv. 1-2), noted his building activity (vv. 2-4), magnified his victory over the Ammonites that was rooted in his godliness (vv. 5-6), and concluded with summary notations as to the source of his reign, his age of accession and length of his reign, and his death, burial, and successor (vv. 7-9). See commentary on 2 Kings 15:32 for an interpretation of his reign.

The Reign of Ahaz (28:1-27)

Length of His Reign and Wickedness (28:1-4)

Ahaz was unqualified in his wickedness and, therefore, soundly condemned by the Chronicler. For specific descriptions of his sin, note commentary on 2 Kings 16:1-20.

God's Punishment of Ahaz and Judah for Ahaz's Wickedness (28:5-8)

"Therefore" (v. 5) indicates that God brought judgment upon Ahaz and Judah for Ahaz's sin. Although the people also sinned, God placed the responsibility of the sin and punishment squarely upon Ahaz, who inspired them in wickedness by his own evil example. In other words, Ahaz should have brought God's blessings upon the people by inspiring them to godly living by his own example. God's judgment took the form of an invasion of Judah by a coalition of Northern Israel and Syria, commonly called the Syro-Ephraimite invasion (vv. 5-8). See commentary on 2 Kings 16:1-20 for Ahaz's refusal of God's gracious offer to save Judah that was delivered to Ahaz by the prophet Isaiah.

Oded the Prophet's Rebuke of Israel (28:9-15)

Oded the prophet, about whom nothing is known, rebuked Israel for venting its rage upon Judah. The Chronicler first noted the message of rebuke (vv. 9-11). The prophet went out to meet the returning army of Israel (v. 9a) and reminded them that they were instruments of God's chastisement of Judah (v. 9b). Then he rebuked them for moving beyond their role as God's instrument of chastisement to venting their wrath upon Judah in slaughtering them (v. 9c) and in enslaving them (v. 10). Next, the prophet pled with the army to repent of their sin and release the captives in order to avoid the fierce wrath of God that was about to be executed on them for their greater sin (v. 11). "Your kinsfolk," which is literally "your brothers," reminded the Israelites of their covenant bond with the people of Judah even though the Northern Kingdom, which soon would be destroyed, stood in rebellion to the house of David. Second, the Chronicler noted the repentant and merciful response of the chiefs of Israel in caring for and releasing the captives of Judah (vv. 12-15).

Ahaz's Unwise Turning to the King of Assyria for Help (28:16-21)

Ahaz sought help from Assyria because of God's further chastisement of Ahaz and Judah in giving them into the hands of the Edomites and the Philistines (vv. 16-19). But the king of Assyria afflicted and brought under vassalage Ahaz and Judah instead of helping them (vv. 20-21). Ahaz's troubles, which compounded themselves at every turn, were all due to his sin (v. 19). Had he been good and faithful instead of wanton and faithless, he would have been secure and prosperous even in the midst of the political cauldron of his day. "Dealt wantonly" means that he by his wickedness allowed lawlessness to run rampant.

Ahaz's Further Apostasy (28:22-25)

Instead of responding to God's chastisement by repenting of his sin, Ahaz plunged deeper into wickedness in turning for help to the gods of Damascus who became the ruin of him and of Judah (vv. 22-23). "This same King Ahaz" (v. 22) puts Ahaz in the class of Athaliah who is called "that wicked woman" (24:7). For his evil actions described in verses 23-25, see commentary on 2 Kings 16:1-20.

Conclusion of His Reign (28:26-27)

The Chronicler noted an additional source to Ahaz's reign (v. 26), his death and ignominious burial (v. 27a), and his successor (v. 27b).

The Reign of Hezekiah (29:1 to 32:33)

The Chronicler's lengthy treatment of Hezekiah is in keeping with his judgment that Hezekiah along with Josiah rivaled even David in being the best of kings. The Chronicler pointed out Hezekiah's failures (32:25,31), but gave him the highest of praise for his wholehearted devotion to God and to his house. In accord with his purpose to magnify the house of God, the Chronicler greatly supplemented Kings in describing

Hezekiah's work in cleansing and reconsecrating the Temple (29:3-36), in the observance of the Passover for all Israel (30:1-27), and in providing for the priesthood and their ministries (31:2-19).

Introductory Observations Concerning His Reign (29:1-2)

The Chronicler noted only the beginning and length of his reign (v. 1a), his mother (v. 1b), and his character (v. 2). Hezekiah began his reign in the last days of the Northern Kingdom. Indeed, the fall of Samaria (722 BC), which brought an end to that kingdom, occurred in the sixth year of his reign. In keeping with his personal godliness and the perilous days of his reign, Hezekiah called the people back to the faith of their fathers. See commentary on 2 Kings 18:1-8 for an interpretation of his godliness, the steps he took to turn Judah back to God, and God's blessings upon his reign.

Restoration of Temple Service (29:3-36)

One of the first steps Hezekiah took to turn the nation back to God was to reopen and repair the doors of the house of God (v. 3), which had been shut by Ahaz his father (28:24). Then he assembled the priests and other Levites from throughout the Land and charged them to sanctify themselves and the house of God for worship in preparation for his restoring the covenant between the Lord and his people (vv. 4-11). The priests and other Levites carried out Hezekiah's desire (vv. 12-19). First, they sanctified themselves, probably by following the instructions of Leviticus 8:5-13 (vv. 12-15a). Second, they sanctified the house of God by removing the trash, by restoring those furnishings that had been removed by Ahaz, and by ceremonially cleansing all of the furnishings of the Temple (vv. 15b-17). Then they reported to Hezekiah that the sanctifying, which involved both cleansing and reconsecrating, had taken place (vv. 18-19). The next step in restoring the Temple service was to reconsecrate to God the royal house, the sanctuary and its servants, and the people. "All Israel" (v. 24) indicates Hezekiah's desire to reconsecrate those of the Northern Kingdom who desired to seek God's face as well as those of Judah. The sin offerings were to atone for their sins. The burnt offerings were to consecrate themselves wholly to the service of God. The burnt offerings were offered on the altar accompanied by the vocal and instrumental praise of the Levitical musicians and the worship of all the people (vv. 25-30). Once the royal house, the sanctuary and its servants, and the people as a whole had been reconsecrated, Hezekiah encouraged the people themselves to offer their sacrifices and thank offerings (v. 31a). Their response was so overwhelming that the priests could not process all of the sacrifices, and other Levites who had sanctified themselves had to help (vv. 31b-35). Hezekiah and the people rejoiced because of the great response God had given in the hearts of the people (v. 36).

Observance of the Passover for All Israel (30:1-27)

Hezekiah sent proclamations of the observance of the Passover feast to all Israel and Judah with an appeal for all of the people of both kingdoms to return to the Lord (vv. 1-9). Hezekiah's appeal was based on God's promises to Solomon concerning forgiveness and restoration for those who would offer penitential prayers in or toward the house of God. See commentary on 2 Chronicles 6:1 to 7:10. Hezekiah's appeal met with meager response in the Northern Kingdom (vv. 10-11), but with overwhelming response in Judah (v. 12). Then the people gathered and observed the Passover and its attendant Feast of Unleavened Bread, with special pardon for those who had not observed rules of cleanness (vv. 13-22). After the observance of the Feast of Unleavened Bread for the prescribed seven days, the whole assembly with great joy and dedication agreed to feast another seven days (v. 23). Hezekiah himself provided the sacrifices (v. 24a). The priests experienced a revival of consecration (v. 24b), and the whole assembly of people were flooded with joy (vv. 25-26). Then the priest and the Levites performed their function of bringing the people to God in prayer, and he heard them in his holy habitation. Thus, the royal house, the sanctuary and its servants, and the people were restored in joyous communion with God. True revival was experienced!

Destruction of the High Places by the People (31:1)

To implement their return to God, the people themselves spontaneously went throughout their Land tearing down the high places. Thus, for the first time in the history of Judah, the high places were destroyed. See comments on 1 Kings 3:1-3 for an interpretation of high places.

Provision for the Priests and Levites and Their Ministries (31:2-19)

Hezekiah organized the priests and other Levites who served at the house of God according to the instructions of David to ensure that there would always be the necessary ministers and ministries at the house of God (v. 2). See commentary on 2 Chronicles 5:11-13 and 8:1-18 for an interpretation of the tasks of the Levites as implemented by David. Hezekiah himself provided the animals for the prescribed burnt offerings (v. 3). Also, he encouraged the people to give "the portion due to the priests and the Levites" (v. 4) so that they could give themselves to their respec-

tive God-ordained ministries. According to the law of Moses, the portion
of the priests and other Levites included the tithe (Num. 18:20-21), the
firstfruits and certain portions of offered sacrifices (Deut. 18:1-5). Mentioned here are the tithes, the firstfruits, and things dedicated to God by
vows (vv. 5-6). Hezekiah seemingly commanded only the people of Jerusalem to bring in the portion due these ministers of God, but when the
word spread the people of Judah and those of the Northern Kingdom
living in Judah responded wholeheartedly so that goods were stockpiled
(vv. 5-10). Hezekiah commanded chambers to be built in the house of
God to store the goods (v. 11; Mal. 3:10), and thereafter the people faithfully brought in the portion of the priests and other Levites (vv. 11-12a).
Also, Hezekiah appointed Levites to oversee the collections (vv. 12b-13),
the freewill offering (v. 14), and the distribution of the goods to the ministers and their families (vv. 15-19).

Evaluation of Hezekiah (31:20-21)

The Chronicler inserted at this point a brief evaluation of Hezekiah.
He noted his good activity throughout Judah (v. 20a), his faithfulness to
the Lord his God (v. 20b), his special devotion to the service of God's
house (v. 21a), and his resultant prosperity (v. 21b).

The Assyrian Invasion (32:1-23)

"After these things and these acts of faithfulness" refers to the faith
and good works of Hezekiah cited above. The Chronicler, thus, put the
Assyrian invasion in its proper perspective. God allowed it to demonstrate Hezekiah's faith and gave Hezekiah the victory because of his
faith. The Chronicler noted: (1) that the king of Assyria sought to con-
quer Judah and her cities for himself (v. 1); (2) Hezekiah's offensive and
defensive measures (vv. 2-8); (3) the contemptuous messages of the king
of Assyria to Hezekiah and the people of Judah (vv. 9-19); (4) Hezekiah's
and Isaiah's prayer to the Lord for help to put to silence the contemptuous Assyrians (v. 20); and (5) the Lord's exalting of himself and his servant Hezekiah by destroying the Assyrian army and bringing death to
the Assyrian king (vv. 21-23). See commentary on 2 Kings 18:9 to 19:37
for a detailed interpretation of the Assyrian aggression.

Hezekiah's Severe Illness, Healing, Pride, and Repentance (32:24-26)

The Chronicler noted briefly: (1) Hezekiah's illness to the point of
death (v. 24a); (2) his prayer for healing (v. 24b); (3) God's sign of healing (v. 24c); (4) Hezekiah's pride that caused God's wrath to come upon
him, Judah, and Jerusalem (v. 25); and (5) his humbling himself along

with the inhabitants of Jerusalem so that God's wrath did not come on them in Hezekiah's day (v. 26). Hezekiah's sinful pride expressed itself in his display of his wealth to the Babylonian envoys (32:31; 2 Kings 20:12-15). See commentary on 2 Kings 20:1-11 for an interpretation of the cause of Hezekiah's illness and of the sign of healing.

Hezekiah's Glory and Honor, but Failures (32:27-31)

The Chronicler noted: (1) Hezekiah's great wealth and honor (vv. 27-29); (2) his wisdom in diverting the Gihon into the city of David (v. 30a); (3) his prosperity in all his works (v. 30b); and (4) his mistake in displaying his glory to the envoys of Babylon (v. 31). See commentary on 2 Kings 20:12-19 for the Babylonian overtures toward Judah and Isaiah's prediction of Babylonian captivity.

Conclusion of His Reign (32:32-33)

The Chronicler noted: (1) additional sources of Hezekiah's reign (v. 32); (2) his death and burial with great honor (v. 33a & b); and (3) his successor (v. 33c). The visions of Isaiah, which were part of the Book of the Kings of Judah and of Israel, probably were additional prophecies of Isaiah not contained in the Book of Isaiah and unknown to us.

The Reign of Manasseh (33:1-20)

Hezekiah, a second David in terms of wholehearted devotion to God, was succeeded by his son Manasseh, who immediately swept away his father's good works and plunged the nation into wickedness. Although the Chronicler for some unknown reason does not say so, the wickedness of Manasseh that characterized his fifty-five year reign up until his conversion late in life led Judah to her destruction (2 Kings 21:10-15; 23:26-27; 24:3). In spite of Manasseh's conversion and his efforts to correct the evil he had loosed and in spite of the personal godliness and reforms of Josiah, wickedness became so ingrained in the people of Judah that only the hard chastisement of exile could correct them.

His Great Wickedness (33:1-10)

After a brief notation concerning the age of Manasseh at his accession and the length of his reign (v. 1), the Chronicler described the apostasy of Manasseh that plunged Judah to the point of no return (vv. 2-10). See commentary on 2 Kings 21:1-18 for interpretation of his apostasy and the result thereof.

His Chastisement by God at the Hands of the King of Assyria (33:11).

"Therefore" indicates that God sent the Assyrian army to punish unrepentant Manasseh and Judah for their sin. "Hooks" and/or nose rings may actually have been used to lead away captives. The language pictures Manasseh as "a wild beast" that had to be subdued and controlled by a hook in its nose (Ezek. 19:4).

His Conversion (33:12-13)

Manasseh illustrated the steps by which a man comes back to God. In his distress he sought God with his whole heart (v. 12a). Also, he prostrated himself before God in humility (v. 12b), and he asked God to save him (v. 13a). God's gracious acceptance and restoration of Manasseh (v. 13b) illustrates how God responds to genuine repentance. "Knew" (v. 13c), which carries the idea of experience, means that Manasseh was convinced by his chastisement, conversion, and restoration that the Lord is God.

His Good Works (33:14-17)

Manasseh also illustrates the good works that flow from genuine conversion. Manasseh, who turned from his own sin, strengthened the fortifications of Jerusalem (v. 14), removed the foreign gods and idols from the house of God (v. 15a), removed all the altars he had built (v. 15b), restored the altar of the Lord and offered upon it sacrifices of peace offerings and of thanksgiving (v. 16a), and commanded the nation to serve the Lord (v. 16b). The people, however, continued to worship in the places of abomination, in spite of his efforts to turn them back to the house of God and to the true altar therein. See commentary on 2 Kings 21:17-18 to note that, although they initially worshiped God at these pagan altars, ultimately they gave themselves wholly over to evil.

Concluding Observations (33:18-20)

The Chronicler noted additional sources of Manasseh's reign (vv. 18-19) and his death, burial, and successor (v. 20). "The Chronicles of the Seers" is the source of Manasseh's conversion and restoration.

The Reign of Amon (33:21-25)

Amon, who continued the apostasy that characterized Manasseh's life before conversion, is briefly treated. The Chronicler noted: (1) the beginning and length of his reign (v. 21); (2) his wickedness after the example of Manasseh his father (v. 22); (3) his failure to repent as his father had done (v. 23); (4) his assassination in his own house at the hands of his servants (v. 24), and (5) his avengers and successor (v. 25). "Did not humble himself" means in light of the total biblical revelation that Amon died unfaithful to God's covenant. Accordingly, Manasseh's sin had at least two tragic consequences: (1) the destruction of his nation and (2) an evil influence on his son.

The Reign of Josiah (34:1 to 35:27)

Josiah, whose name means "the Lord heals," sought to bring healing to his nation. Like his great-grandfather Hezekiah, Josiah rivaled even David in godliness. Also, he vigorously pressed religious reforms upon the people in hopes of turning Judah from the wickedness that swamped them during most of the fifty-seven years of Manasseh and Amon. Josiah, however, could not save the nation. Evil was so entrenched in the people that they immediately returned to wickedness at his death (2 Kings 23:32).

Introductory Observations (34:1-2)

The Chronicler noted the beginning and length of Josiah's reign (v. 1) and his devotion to the Lord after the example of David his father (v. 2). See commentary on 2 Kings 18:1-8 for a comparison of the faith of Josiah with that of Hezekiah.

Initial Steps in Reformation (34:3-7)

Josiah began to seek the Lord (was converted) in the eighth year of his reign, that is, at sixteen years of age (v. 3a). He began to purge Judah and Jerusalem of false religions in the twelfth year of his reign, that is, when he was twenty years old (vv. 3b-7).

His Repair of the House of the Lord (34:8-13)

Josiah began his great reformation in his eighteenth year, that is, when he was twenty-six years of age, with the repair of the Temple. The Chronicler first noted the time of and leaders involved in the repair of the Temple (v. 8). Then he recorded how the money for the repair of the house of God, which had been collected from the people, was given to the overseers of the workmen for materials and labor (vv. 9-11). Finally, he noted the faithful labor of the workmen and their overseers (vv. 12-13). See commentary on 2 Kings 22:3-8.

Hilkiah's Discovery of the Book of the Law (34:14-18)

While collecting from the chests the money to be used in the repair, Hilkiah the high priest discovered "the book of the law of the Lord given through Moses" (v. 14). "The book of the law" was at least Deuteronomy and possibly the first five books of the Bible. See commentary on 2 Kings 22:3-8. The Chronicler noted the discovery by Hilkiah (v. 14), Hilkiah's giving the book to Shaphan to deliver to the king (v. 15), Shaphan's bringing the book to the king and reporting on the repair of the Temple (vv. 16-18a), and Shaphan's reading to the king from the book (v. 18b).

Josiah's Repentance and Call of Israel to Obedience (34:19-28)

Josiah repented in response to the reading of the book of the law and sought to call the people of Judah and Israel to obedience. The king rent his clothes to symbolize his deep grief and repentance over the sins of the people and the promised curses of God for their sin (v. 19). Then the king commanded a delegation to inquire of the Lord concerning the fate of himself and of the Israelites yet remaining in the Land (vv. 20-21). The delegation went to Huldah the prophetess (v. 22) and brought back a twofold message from God: (1) because of their sin, God would bring upon the Land and upon the remaining people all of the curses written in the book (vv. 23-25); but (2) God would not execute these curses in the day of Josiah because of Josiah's repenting at the reading of God's Word (vv. 26-28). See commentary on 2 Kings 22:9-20.

Josiah's Leading the People to Obey the Covenant (34:29-33)

Josiah was not content with the promise that the desolation of the Land, the Temple, and the people would not occur in his day. He sought new life for the nation by bringing the people to a renewal of the covenant with the Lord. See commentary on 2 Kings 23:1-20, and 11:17-20 for an interpretation of the covenant into which they entered and of Josiah's reforms. "Made all who were in Israel serve the Lord their God" (v. 33) seemingly tells the story of Josiah's reformation. Although the people followed the Lord all the days of Josiah from external pressure, they never came to the point of serving God out of personal love for him. Their hearts were still wedded to sin.

His Observance of the Passover (35:1-19)

Josiah climaxed his great reformation in the eighteenth year of his reign with the observance of the Passover exactly according to the law of

Moses (v. 18). See commentary on 2 Kings 23:21-33. He observed the Passover at the time prescribed by Moses (v. 1). Josiah reorganized the priests and other Levites to carry out their functions according to the law of Moses (vv. 2-6). "Put the holy ark in the house" (v. 3) indicates that the ark had been removed from the Temple by the Levites for its protection, probably during the wicked reigns of Manasseh and Amon. Josiah, his princes, the chief officers of the house of God, and the chiefs of the Levites willingly provided the sacrificial animals (vv. 7-9). Then they observed the Passover according to the law of Moses (vv. 10-15). The concluding notations magnify the distinctiveness of their observance of the Passover (vv. 16-19). Note, however, the absence of any remark indicating that genuine revival took place. Contrast the statement of Hezekiah's day that the voice of the priests and Levites in prayer for the people was heard by God (2 Chron. 30:27). The revival in Hezekiah's day brought the nation back to God. They could have moved on from there to special blessings. But the wickedness of Manasseh, the son and successor of Hezekiah, sealed their doom.

His Death in the Battle against Pharaoh Neco and Concluding Observations (35:20-27)

The Chronicler in this section supplemented Kings: (1) by adding details of Josiah's fatal battle; and (2) by explaining that good king Josiah died at the hands of Neco because of Josiah's refusal to hear the word of God that came through Neco. See commentary on 2 Kings 23:28-30. "The Laments," which contained the lamentations of Jeremiah and others for Josiah, no longer exists. Our Book of Lamentations, which is entirely separate, perhaps illustrates the nature of the lamentations.

The Reigns of Jehoahaz, Jehoiakim, and Jehoiachin (36:1-10)

The Reign of Jehoahaz (36:1-4)

The Chronicler moved swiftly through the reigns of the remaining kings of Judah to the Exile with a greatly abbreviated version of 2 Kings 23:31 to 25:30. The people reflected their evil nature in replacing Josiah at his untimely death with Jehoahaz, a wicked son of Josiah, who immediately reverted to the evil practices of Manasseh, Amon, and other wicked kings of Judah (v. 1). See commentary on 2 Kings 23:31-35. The

Chronicler noted merely the beginning and length of Jehoahaz's reign (v. 2) and that Jehoahaz was deposed and deported to Egypt by the king of Egypt (vv. 3-4). The king of Egypt, who imposed heavy tribute on the land of Judah, appointed Jehoahaz's brother, whose name he changed to Jehoiakim, to reign over Judah.

The Reign of Jehoiakim (36:5-8)

The captivity of Judah in Babylon began with the wicked reign of Jehoiakim (Dan. 1:1). See commentary on 2 Kings 23:36 to 24:7 for details. The Chronicler noted the beginning and length of his reign (v. 5a), his wickedness (v. 5b), his enslavement by Nebuchadnezzar king of Babylon (vv. 6-7), and concluding observations concerning Jehoiakim's reign (v. 8). Whether Jehoiakim was actually taken to Babylon is not known. Perhaps, Nebuchadnezzar merely bound him in chains to scare him into submission. However, "also" (v. 7) seems to imply that Nebuchadnezzar took Jehoiakim to Babylon along with the vessels of the house of God.

The Reign of Jehoiachin (36:9-10)

The second stage of the Babylonian captivity occurred during and cut short the wicked reign of Jehoiachin. See commentary on 2 Kings 24:8-17 for details. "Eight years old" (v. 9) probably should read "eighteen years old" (2 Kings 24:8). See commentary on 2 Kings 25:27-30 for the significance of the royal treatment given to Jehoiachin in the thirty-seventh year of his captivity by Evil-merodach.

The Reign of Zedekiah: Final Stage of Exile (36:11-21)

The final stage of the Babylonian captivity, which included the destruction of Jerusalem, ransacking and burning of the Temple, and deportation of the remaining people, occurred in the eleventh year of Zedekiah. God did everything he could to bring them to repentance and, thus, to avoid the desolation of the people, the Land, and the house of God. The Chronicler noted: (1) the beginning and length of Zedekiah's reign (v. 11); his wickedness (vv. 12-13); (3) the wickedness of his leading priests and of his people (v. 14); (4) their fatal sin in failing to heed the messengers of God urging them to repent (vv. 15-16); and (5) their death, destruction, and Exile at the hands of the Babylonians (vv. 17-21). See commentary on 2 Kings 24:18 to 25:21. The desolation was in accord with the promised curses of disobedience (Lev. 26:31-33) and in fulfillment of the prophecy of Jeremiah (Jer. 25:8-10). "Until the land had enjoyed its sabbaths" (v. 21) also goes back to the promised desolation (Lev. 26:34-35). The land would enjoy rest during the desolation to make up for their violation of Moses' command to give the land a year of rest every seventh year. The desolation was seventy years to fulfill Jeremiah's prophecy (Jer. 25:11-12). "Until the establishment of the kingdom of Persia" (v. 20) has meaning in light of Isaiah's prophecy that the Medo-Persian Empire would destroy Babylon (Isa. 13:17-22). "Until" (vv. 20-21) and "to fulfill seventy years" (v. 21) pointed to the new day for God's people when he would bring them back into the Land in fulfillment of his promises (Jer. 25:12; 29:10-14; Lev. 25:40-45).

Appendix: The Decree of Cyrus to Rebuild the House of God (36:22-23)

This passage is essentially repeated in Ezra 1:1-4. Probably, it was added here after 1 and 2 Chronicles were accepted as canonical and placed as the last two books in the Hebrew Bible. The purpose for adding it was twofold: (1) to end the Old Testament on a note of hope; and (2) to indicate that the scribal interpretation of the history of Israel found in 1 and 2 Chronicles was continued in Ezra and Nehemiah.

The decree of Cyrus urging the Jews in captivity to return to Jerusalem to rebuild the house of God came in the providence of God in the first year of Cyrus's reign. It came at that time to fulfill the prophecy of Jeremiah concerning their returning to the Land after seventy years in captivity (Jer. 25:11-12; 29:10-14; cf. Isa. 44:28).

The seventy years are figured in different ways, the most likely being from the first stage of captivity in 605 BC to 536 BC, the first year of Cyrus's reign. The Chronicler noted: (1) the date of the decree (v. 22a); (2) the purpose of the decree (v. 22b); (3) the motivating force of the decree (v. 22c); and (4) the substance of Cyrus's decree (v. 23). The substance of Cyrus's decree is that God, who had given Cyrus all the kingdoms of the earth, had charged him to build him a house in Jerusalem by liberating the people of God to return to Jerusalem to do the work. Accordingly, the scribal interpretation of the history of Israel ends in Chronicles and continues in Ezra and Nehemiah, magnifying the house of God in Jerusalem upon which God had set his name forever (2 Chron. 7:16; 1 Kings 9:3).

Bibliography

General Works

Childs, Brevard S. *Introduction to the Old Testament as Scripture.* Philadelphia: Fortress Press, 1979.

Driver, S. R. *An Introduction to the Literature of the Old Testament.* Edinburgh: T. and T. Clark, 1891.

Watts, J. Wash. *Old Testament Teaching.* Nashville: Broadman Press, 1967.

Young, Edward J. *An Introduction to the Old Testament.* Grand Rapids: Wm. B. Eerdmans Publishing Co., 1953.

Commentaries

Allen, Clifton J., Gen. Ed. *The Broadman Bible Commentary*, Vol. 3. Nashville: Broadman Press, 1970.

Buttrick, George Arthur, Gen. Ed. *The Interpreter's Bible*, Vol. 3. New York: Abingdon Press, 1954.

Crockett, William Day. *A Harmony of Samuel, Kings and Chronicles.* Grand Rapids: Baker Book House, 1951.

Curtis, Edward Lewis and Madsen, Albert Alonzo. *The International Critical Commentary: The Books of Chronicles.* Edinburgh: T. and T. Clark, 1910.

Gray, John. *The Old Testament Library: 1 and 2 Kings.* Philadelphia: The Westminster Press, 1964.

Keil, C. F. and Delitzsch, F. *Biblical Commentaries on the Old Testament*, Vol. 6. Grand Rapids: Wm. B. Eerdmans Publishing Co., 1950.

Keil, C. F. and Delitzsch, F. *Biblical Commentaries on the Old Testament*, Vol. 7. Grand Rapids: Wm. B. Eerdmans Publishing Co., 1950.

Lumby, J. Rawson. *The Cambridge Bible for Schools and Colleges: The*

First Books of the Kings. Cambridge: At the University Press, 1892).

Lumby, J. Rawson. *The Cambridge Bible for Schools and Colleges: The Second Book of Kings.* Cambridge: At the University Press, 1891.

McGee, J. Vernon. *1 and 2 Kings.* Pasadena, California: Thru the Bible Books, 1976.

Montgomery, James A. and Gehman, Henry Snyder. *The International Critical Commentary: The Books of Kings.* Edinburgh: T. and T. Clark, 1951.

Myers, Jacob M. *The Anchor Bible: II Chronicles.* Garden City, N.Y.: Doubleday and Company, Inc., 1965.

Dictionaries, Encyclopedias, and Lexicons

Brown, Francis, Driver, S. R., and Briggs, Charles A. *A Hebrew and English Lexicon of the Old Testament.* Oxford: At the Clarendon Press, 1907.

Buttrick, George Arthur, Ed. *The Interpreter's Dictionary of the Bible.* New York: Abingdon Press, 1962.

Davis, John D. and Gehman, Henry S. *The Westminster Dictionary of the Bible.* Philadelphia: The Westminster Press, 1944.

Dentan, Robert C. *The Layman's Bible Commentary: The First and Second Books of the Kings and The First and Second Books of the Chronicles.* Atlanta, Georgia: John Knox Press, 1964.

Kittel, Rud. *Biblia Hebraica.* Stuttgart: Privileg. Wiirtt. Bibelanstalt, 1937.

Orr, James, Ed. *The International Standard Bible Encyclopedia.* Grand Rapids: Wm. B. Eerdmans Publishing Co., 1930.

Tenny, Merrill C. *The Zondervan Pictorial Encyclopedia of the Bible.* Grand Rapids: Zondervan Publishing House, 1975.

Tregelles, Samuel Prideaux. *Gesenius' Hebrew and Chaldee Lexicon.* Grand Rapids: Wm. B. Eerdmans Publishing Company, 1952.